BRITAIN IN OLD PHOTOGRAPHS

IRISH MANCHESTER REVISITED

Alan Keegan & Danny Claffey

Title page photograph: St Brendan's under-14s, Lancashire Champions, 1997.

First published 2013

The History Press
The Mill, Brimscombe Port
Stroud, Gloucestershire, GL5 2QG
www.thehistorypress.co.uk

© Alan Keegan & Danny Claffey, 2013

The right of Alan Keegan & Danny Claffey to be identified as the Authors of this work has been asserted in accordance with the Copyrights, Designs and Patents Act 1988.

All rights reserved. No part of this book may be reprinted or reproduced or utilised in any form or by any electronic, mechanical or other means, now known or hereafter invented, including photocopying and recording, or in any information storage or retrieval system, without the permission in writing from the Publishers.

British Library Cataloguing in Publication Data.
A catalogue record for this book is available from the British Library.

ISBN 978 0 7524 8816 5

Typesetting and origination by The History Press
Printed in Great Britain

CONTENTS

	About the Authors	4
	Introduction	6
1	Shorrocks Palais Royal Irish Club & Ardri Irish Club	7
2	Pubs & Clubs	21
3	Bands, Singers & Entertainers	31
4	Irish Dancing & Traditional Music	39
5	Irish World Heritage Centre & Irish Community Care (Rose Morris)	59
6	Irish County Associations (Manchester)	79
7	St Ann's GAA (Stretford) 1999–2009	89
8	Sport	101
9	People & Places	109
	Acknowledgements	128

ABOUT THE AUTHORS

A group on the christening day of Alan Keegan, photographed on Welby Street, Chorlton-on-Medlock, which was situated off Hathersage Road (High Street). In the background is the tower of Victoria swimming baths. Alan was born in 1962 and is the youngest of five children. His parents Felix and Margaret (also known as 'Dotie') originated from County Leitrim. Alan has held a number jobs which have included media and sport and he is currently a principal lecturer at the University of Central Lancashire, Preston. He supports the team which has won the Premier League more times than any other, Manchester United. Left to right: Seamus Keegan, Madge Keegan (Duffy) holding baby Damian Rafferty, Maura Keegan (née Rafferty) holding baby Alan Keegan, while at the front is Padraig Keegan, July 1962.

Danny Claffey was born in December 1947 in Prestbury, Cheshire. His parents who came from Westmeath and Donegal brought up their five children in the Withington area of Manchester. Danny attended St Gregory's Technical High School in Ardwick, leaving at the age of sixteen. Various jobs followed such as shop assistant, labourer and gardener until he went off to Australia in 1970 with his pal Jimmy McCafferty. Three years later Danny returned to Manchester and a year later was married to Susan. They have three children, Patrick, Erin and Oliver (also known as Jack). Danny worked for British Gas for twenty years and started taking photographs in his spare time for the *Irish Post* in 1984 and still does to this day. He is an avid supporter and season ticket holder of Manchester's top Premiership team, Manchester City, and likes a drop of Jameson's now and again. Back, left to right: Mary Claffey; Margaret McGonagle; Mary B. Gallagher; Mary-Anne Gallagher; Danny Claffey; John, Catherine and Pat O'Brien. Front: Tony Gallagher; Thomas and Mary O'Brien, June 1948.

INTRODUCTION

Welcome to this third volume of *Irish Manchester* in the 'Britain in Old Photographs' series. As with the first two books, we have delved into the past to give you a glimpse of what Manchester's Irish community and their families and friends were getting involved in, mostly in their social, sport and leisure time.

Many of you may remember some of the old Irish dance halls depicted in the book; you may have danced in one of the places or even met your partner in one of the popular establishments. The Irish settlers in Manchester have always been a very sociable, gregarious group, which you will witness for yourself in the many historic photographs inside. Many of the Irish pubs and clubs where the photographs were taken have now long gone or have been demolished, but memories live long.

If you live or have lived in the Manchester area you may find a photo of yourself, but if not, you will more than likely find a relative or old friend on one of the pages. Many people in the book are no longer with us, while many depicted as children are now in their thirties, forties or fifties and have their own families. It doesn't matter where you are from or what age you are, take a peek into the past and see how the Manchester Irish helped to make the city as vibrant as it is today. *Irish Manchester Revisited* is a true reflection of our community in Manchester.

Alan Keegan & Danny Claffey, 2013

1

SHORROCKS PALAIS ROYAL IRISH CLUB & ARDRI IRISH CLUB

Jim Connell standing at the entrance to Shorrocks on Brunswick Street, 1960s.

SHORROCKS PALAIS ROYAL & THE NEW ARDI IRISH CLUB

Jim Connell was born in Ballyhaunis, County Mayo, and his wife Mona was born in Ballaghaderreen, County Roscommon. Jim and Mona Connell started the Shorrocks Palais Royal Irish Club, which was situated at 199 Brunswick Street, in 1952 and ran it until 1963/4 when it was taken over by Manchester University. They then converted the King's Cinema which was situated at 509 Stockport Road, Longsight, and started another popular venue which was called the Ardri Irish Club. This was later relocated to Coupland Street in Hulme and known as the New Ardri.

Jim Connell was a man who did many great things for the Irish community in Manchester, such as fundraising activities and charity dances which in many cases would help families where the father had been in a fatal accident at work. There is a story where the widow of a family had no groceries or lightbulbs in the house. Jim heard about the unfortunate woman, and even though it was late in the evening he went and bought her what she needed. There were many examples of where the charity dance money paid for the funerals of Irish people who had fallen upon hard times.

Jim was also very friendly with a nun called Sister Patrick from a convent in Victoria Park who with her fellow nuns fed and clothed many people from the Victoria Park and Rusholme areas. Jim helped the nuns in many ways including introducing them to contacts and influential business friends such as Leslie Lever MP. At Christmas time he would drive Sister Patrick to the big stores and shops in Manchester such as Lewis's, C&A, Marks & Spencers and Henry's, to name a few. The stores would donate clothes, shoes, food and other items which would be collected in a van arranged by Jim and taken to the convent.

For many years a lovely elderly English lady called Mrs Burnside, who lived in Westwood Street in Moss Side, worked in the tea bar (no alcohol in those days) of the Shorrocks. She was like a mother to all the Irish people who came into the dance hall. One night the fog was really bad in Manchester and Jim had great difficulty getting to the hall to open up; however, on his arrival he was surprised to see Mrs Burnside waiting at the door, having walked all the way in the thick fog. She was also the only help to turn up that night.

There are many great memories and stories from the Shorrocks and Ardri. It used to be 3s 6d to gain entry. Later in 1960 it would cost 6s on a night when a special band or singer from Ireland was performing. Performers and singers who appeared at the Shorrocks Palais Royal included Val Doonican, the Big Four (whose lead singer Pat McGuigan was the father of boxer Barry McGuigan), the Bachelors in 1960 and the Capitol Show Band with lead singer Brendan Boyer of 'Hucklebuck' fame.

Jim also organised dances in many other towns and venues over the years. He rented the New Century Hall one year for New Year's Eve and had Joe Loss and his Orchestra performing on the night! Jim ran the New Ardri Club for many years until Tom McKenna took it over in 1982. He then moved back to Ballaghaderreen in Roscommon and sadly passed away in 1997.

The Association of Ballrooms Limited certificate for the Shorrocks Palais Royal.

A promotional leaflet for an event at the Guildhall, Londonderry, on 15 August 1959. Jim Connell presents Des Byrne and his fabulous Skyliners, billed as 'a 14-piece show band from the principal Irish ballroom in Manchester'.

The 'cash box'. Left to right: Jim Connell, Kathleen Connell and John Connell.

At Christmas 1964, behind the bar we see Winnie Manning and Kathleen Connell.

The Shorrocks' resident band – the Skyliners.

The Skyliners – standing at the microphone are lead singer Joe Kennedy and Tommie Owens.

The 1958 Shorrocks Beauty Queen Kathleen Keaveney with, among others, Jim Connell, Kathleen Connell and lead singer Joe Kennedy. Joe Kennedy and Kathleen Keaveney were married in January 1960.

Jim and Mona Connell, -?-, the 1960 Beauty Queen and Kathleen Connell.

A group shot of Shorrocks beauty pageant contestants.

Peggy McCabe and Kathleen Connell are seen in this 1962 photograph of a beauty pageant at Shorrocks.

Shorrocks beauty queens.

Jim Connell and the Ballroom Beauty Queen holding her prize.

Tommie Owens, Des Byrne and five beautiful young ladies who were enjoying a night out at the Shorrocks.

Jim Connell and Tommie Owens present prizes to these four lucky ladies.

Two girls enjoying a night out at the Shorrocks.

Seen here with Jim Connell are Pat Moylet, Austin Hopkins and Babe Connell.

The famous Gallowglass Ceili Band were one of the many popular acts to entertain at the Shorrocks.

The popular Sheba Kelly and her all-female band seen here with Jim Connell at the Shorrocks in the 1960s.

The singing star Michael Holliday is seen here with Jim and Mona Connell, Tommie Owens and Des Byrne. Seated on the couch with Michael are Mona Reynolds (sister of famous Gaelic footballer Mick Reynolds) and Kathleen Connell.

Seen here are, left to right: Pat Connell, Michael Connell, John Connell, Frank Dolan, -?-, Jim Connell.

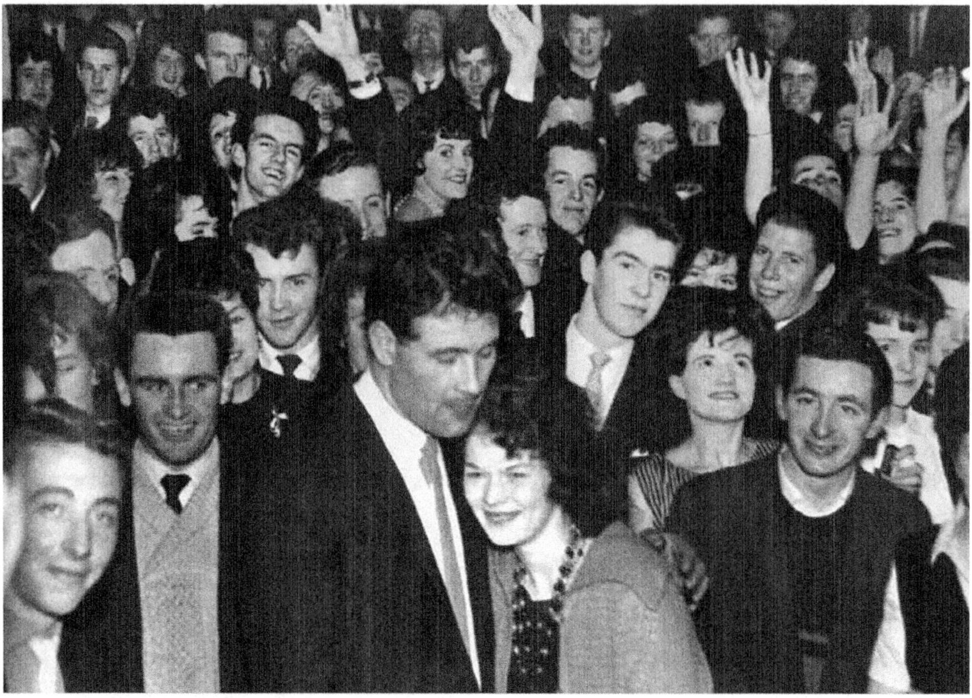

Another full house at the Shorrocks, 1960s.

Shorrocks

★ PALAIS ROYAL IRISH CLUB ★

Brunswick Street (Nr University) Manchester 13

FRIDAY, 29th January

★ *SPECIAL ATTRACTION*

The Fabulous . . .

CAPITOL SHOWBAND

IRELAND'S GREATEST ATTRACTION

Currently appearing at the London Palladium & T.V.

SATURDAY, 30th January

★ **Another big attraction**

THE BANSHEES SHOWBAND

★ **Dancing** *from* **8 p.m.** *to* **2 a.m.** ★

● FULLY LICENSED BAR ● Special Late Transport to all parts

We have now acquired new premises . . .

THE KING'S CINEMA, 509 STOCKPORT RD, Longsight, Mc 13

which has been converted into a luxurious IRISH CLUB to be known as . . .

THE ARBRI IRISH CLUB

● OPENING IN THE VERY NEAR FUTURE ●

APPLY FOR MEMBERSHIP to 509 Stockport Road, or Palais Royal Irish Club, 199 Brunswick St

— *Large Car Park at Rear* —

Buses : From Piccadilly 92, 93, 94, 95, 96 — From Albert Sq 85, 89 — 53

S. Brown, 518 Claremont Rd., Manchester 14

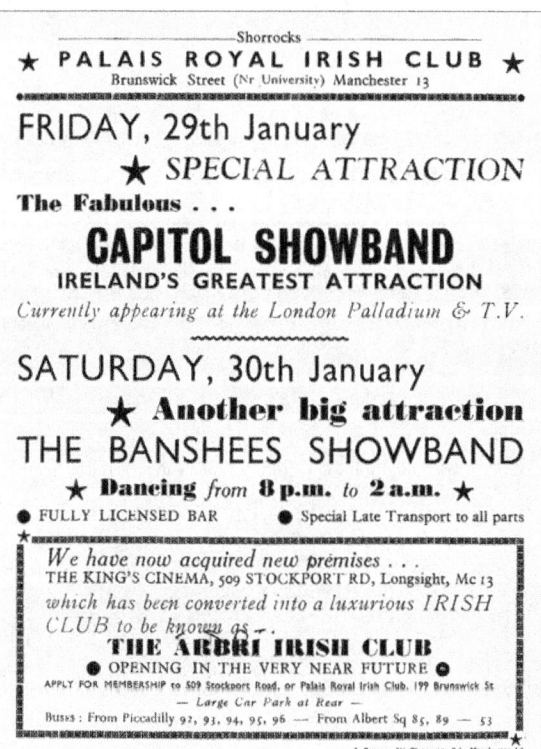

Leaflet promoting the fabulous Capitol Showband – 'Ireland's Greatest Attraction' – and the Banshees Showband. The leaflet also mentions that the Shorrocks had acquired new premises, the King's Cinema on 599 Stockport Road, Longsight, M13. This was the Ardri Irish Club (Ardri is Gaelic for King).

The Ardri dance hall staff including Mary Ging, Ann Hopkins, Joan Arlington (Jim's secretary), Pat McNally and Josie Duncan.

Seen here at the Ardri are Jim Connell, singer and TV star Joe Lynch and Bill Gallagher, the Princess pub manager.

Two girls' nights out at the Ardri Irish Club, 1970s.

Jim Connell and friends at the Ardri.

2

PUBS & CLUBS

The New Ardri on Coupland Street is now long gone, but was very popular in its day.

Norah and Tom Dunican pictured with staff and friends behind the bar of the Little Western Pub in 1984. The name was later changed to Dunican's Bar.

In August 1989 the Grove Club was launched in Plymouth Grove, Longsight, by Michael and Della Costello, who are pictured here with family and friends on the opening night. Della is seated centre and Michael is standing second from right.

Pictured here are Kevin Lane, Damien Lestrange, Vanessa Rudden, Martin Blyth and Rachel Jones enjoying a night out at the 32 Club in Ardwick, August 1996.

The winners of the Manchester Irish Festival Pub Quiz in 1996 were these brainy people from the popular Albert pub, Wilmslow Road, Withington.

In September 1994 the English Martyrs Parish Centre celebrated its 21st anniversary with a big celebration at the popular venue in Whalley Range. Pictured here are members of the original committee who worked so hard to get the club going and made it as popular as it is today. Left to right: Tony Warnock, John Brennan, George O'Neill, Martin Maloney and John Tully.

Enjoying a sportsman's evening at the Grove Club in the early 1990s are Jimmy Wagg of Radio Manchester Sport, Bernard Lofthouse, Tracy Costello, Sir Alex Ferguson and Michael Costello.

Miss Carousel, February 1969. Maureen Lynott (née McDonagh), Ignatius Lynott, Winnie McDonagh (Miss Carousel 1969 who won 100 guineas and was from Ballina, County Mayo), Kathleen McAloon, Kay McDonagh. Kay McDonagh was the runner-up and Kathleen McDonald came in third place.

A night out at the New Ardri in August 1985. Seen here are Teresa Coen, Marion Connolly, Mary Daly, Mick Connolly, Susan Conroy, Tommy Coen and Sean Daly.

Seamus Feeley, Paddy Joe Walsh and Pat Feeley were all regulars at the Astoria Ballroom on Richmond Grove in the mid-1960s when this photo was taken. Their furry companion was also a regular at the Astoria with his photographer friend.

In February 2000 the Irish folk in Bolton opened their own Irish Centre when they took over the old Nightingale pub and converted it into a compact, homely club. Pictured here on the opening night are, left to right: Jimmy McSharry, Kevin Gargan, Brendan O'Doherty and Michael Sherlock. If you look closely you will see that they are all sporting cardboard bow-ties which they made especially for the occasion.

The official opening of the Irish World Heritage Centre in Cheetham Hill, November 1986. Five-month-old Clare Hennessy was the youngest guest at the opening of the new centre, pictured here with her mother, Eileen.

Members of the Mayo Youth Organisation at their fancy dress dance which was held at the Irish World Heritage Centre in November 1984.

The old Denmark pub which was situated on the corner of Lloyd Street and Denmark Road. It was a popular meeting place for the local Irish workers in the 1950s.

The Horseshoe pub on Chapel Street in Levenshulme, always a popular haunt of the local Irish population.

Mulligans pub just off Deansgate in the city centre.

The Southern hotel/pub on the corner of Nell Lane and Mauldeth Road in Chorlton was a very good music venue and also hosted many Irish weddings over the years.

The Union Inn on Stockport Road, Levenshulme – a well-known Irish haunt.

The Bowling Green on Brookburn Road in Chorlton-cum-Hardy.

The Whalley Hotel at Brooks Bar in Whalley Range has been a meeting place for the Irish community since the early 1950s.

O'Shea's Irish Bar on Whitworth Street is one of the most popular Irish pubs in Manchester – a great venue for live music and sports.

The Victoria Inn on Burnage Lane is another popular Irish-run hostelry.

St Edward's Confraternity Club on Great Western Street in Rusholme.

Dancing in St Brendan's Club, City Road, in the early 1990s.

At St Brendan's Club on City Road in 1984 are, among others, Ann Mannion, John Murphy and Steve Mannion.

At St Brendan's in the 1970s are Philomena Murphy, Nora Rabbette, Ted, Denis Murphy, Tommy Quirk, Teresa Gaffney and Eddie Rabbette.

3

BANDS, SINGERS & ENTERTAINERS

Here we see two old stalwarts of the Irish music scene spanning many, many years in the pubs and clubs of Manchester. Paddy Feery and Mick Breen are both sadly no longer with us, but their musical legacy still lives on.

The late Bernard Cooke, playing at the time with the Champions Showband, at a Galway Association dance in Our Lady's Hall, Moss Side, 1985.

The 1992 line-up of Manchester band Pat Jordan and Finian's Rainbow. Here we see Steve Flynn, Tony Corrigan, Chris Reilly, Kieran Towey and Pat Jordan.

A youthful Aiden Kennedy and the Strangers, including Mike O'Brien, Billy Regan, Hughie Cummins and Duncan Mulvey, pictured here at a Manchester gig in 1986.

Local Manchester band Ceile pictured here backstage in 1995. Colin Farrell, Colin Harries, Eamonn Dinan, Nathan Finn and Ged Stenson are all fine musicians.

Samantha Morris and Tony Howley belting out a few reels at a fireside session in St Kentigern's Irish Club, September 1998.

Pipe Major Frank Judge and his daughter Sarah at an Irish World Heritage Centre's piper's fundraising dance in 1997.

The 1998 line-up of one of Manchester's finest ever bands, Toss the Feathers.

Musician and singer Sean Brady, Paddy McElherron, Sean Kennedy, Mike Kelly and Cathal Daly are pictured here outside the Mountain Dew record shop which was on Claremont Road in Moss Side back in the 1980s.

Enjoying the Manchester Irish Bands Association dinner at the Irish World Heritage Centre in 1994 were Marcella and Eddie Byrne, Marie and Val Turner, Brendan and Bernie Forkan.

In October 1986 the Carousel Ballroom on Plymouth Grove reopened for a time. Top of the bill at the reopening was Larry Cunningham and his band the Mighty Avons.

Saturday nights at the New Ardri were always nights to remember. Pictured here in the centre is singer Seamus Moore relaxing with friends before going on stage, 1993.

Ned Brennan, Mary and Peter Holland and Eddie Sweeney are seen here at a Manchester Irish Bands Association dinner at the Irish World Heritage Centre in 1995.

Clare Music Festival at St Kentigern's Club in 1998. All those pictured were medal- and trophy-winners in the various competitions. Front row: Natalie Bromley and Claire Simpson. Middle row: Charlotte Earley, Jennifer Noone and Patricia O'Grady. Back row: Joe McPartland, Patricia McEnroe and Christopher Booth.

Piper and flautist Mike McGoldrick playing at the Northern Regional Ceili at St Kentigern's Club in 1995. Over the years Mike has been a member of several influential bands. In 1994 he was awarded the BBC Young Tradition Award and in 2001 he was given the Instrumentalist of the Year award at the BBC Radio 2 Folk Awards. These days he appears regularly with artistes such as Mark Knopfler and Sharon Shannon on their tours.

Established in 1994, the band Skidoo was begun by Longford musician Peter Carberry who had already founded Toss the Feathers among others a few years earlier. Peter is seated on the stairs in a black leather jacket.

The band Quare Craic have been going for many years now. Singer, guitarist and actor Kieran Cunningham has always been lead singer, but over the years there has been a change of musicians at various times. Pictured here in Mulligan's in 1997 are Andy Jones, Kieran Cunningham and Dezi Donnelly.

Over 500 guests attended the Irish Abroad Charitable Trust dinner at Mere Golf Club in November 1998. Chief guest was songwriter and pianist Phil Coulter pictured here with Manchester's own Eamonn O'Neal, radio and TV producer and director.

John Coleman is seen here on the accordion in the centre playing with the old St Chad's Ceili Band back in the 1950s.

Enjoying the Manchester Irish Bands Association's annual dinner at the Grove Club in 1997 are Rose West, Pat Jordan and Evelyn Bergin.

Manchester Irish Radio presenter Marian Waldron with Foster and Allen. They were the special guests who officially opened the station in 1994.

4

IRISH DANCING & TRADITIONAL MUSIC

Taken at the first ever Langley Feis in north Manchester. Among those gathered are Regina Grainger, Fr John Murphy, John Barlow Snr, Tom Brophy, Brenda Grainger, John Boyd, Mrs Neary, Mrs Noonan and Mrs O'Rourke.

GRAINGER SCHOOL OF IRISH DANCING

Brenda, Regina and Maureen Grainger

Perhaps the most natural progression after spending many happy years learning and perfecting the art and joys of Irish traditional dancing was to share that knowledge and enjoyment with others. On the invitation of Canon John Murphy, P.P. Our Lady of the Assumption, Langley, and prompted by the happy occasion of Maureen Grainger having just won the Ladies' All-Ireland Senior Championship – the first person to win this award outside Ireland – our Irish traditional dancing school commenced in 1957 in his school hall.

His large parish consisted of many hardworking families who had been relocated from inner-city areas and who were anxious to give their children the opportunity to learn and explore the culture of their homeland. So began the story and delightful endeavours of the Grainger School of Irish Dancing. Under Canon Murphy's leadership, Langley Feis was introduced which encompassed many forms of Irish culture – such as singing, elocution, choral, dancing, etc. – and it was at these annual festivals that choreography competitions were first introduced. Who could ever forget the 'Finnegan's Wake' choreographed by Margaret O'Neal?

Our dancing schools soon expanded across Manchester and Stockport in areas where there was an acute need for recreation for teenagers and children alike. During the early years, our dancers participated in numerous events, some of which were for Fr Ignatius Tierney of St Clare's, Blackley, who organised the then famous Houldsworth Hall, Manchester, and St George's Hall, Liverpool, St Patrick's week celebrations, for which their reward was a tour of the Cavern in Liverpool, home club of the Beatles and a very hearty lunch at the Convent of Mercy, Liverpool! How times change!

Following the retirement of Fr Ignatius in 1971, we continued to compete in all the major and minor competitions and city halls throughout Ireland, England and Scotland. Our pursuits were by no means confined to competition; at least half of our dancing days were spent in support of our local charities and functions which formed a very large part of life in Manchester in those years. Every Whit Friday we had the joy of endeavouring to walk smartly down Market Street, Manchester, behind the excellent Brian Boru pipe band of St Brigid's, in support of the 'Faith of our Fathers'.

During 1972 we were invited by Leeds University to be a part of their folk dancing group to display and teach Irish dancing to groups of students from continental Europe. This was a most wonderful opportunity for us to impart our knowledge of Irish traditional dancing and music to a much wider audience. They, in turn, were enthralled by the grace and intricacies of our Irish cultural performances, each country being eager to learn from us. We were very proud to have been chosen to do so.

During the following twenty years we travelled extensively, sometimes two or three times per year during school and college holidays, throughout Holland, Germany, Hungary, Austria, Czechoslovakia, Turkey, Poland, Spain, France and Belgium. I am sure you will agree that this was a dimension beyond competition which did not require trophies and medals, as we endeavoured to take Irish dancing out of its traditional isolation at that period of time and offer it for appreciation to the greater and more extensive audience. It was also of immense educational value to our pupils.

1979 brought the Independence of Malta when we were invited to take part in their celebrations which involved many heads of state and we felt honoured to be representing Irish culture at such a level. For this and for exhibiting internationally, we were presented with the Irish Post Community Award of 1979 by the then Irish Ambassador, Dr Eamonn Kennedy at the Royal Garden Hotel, Kensington, an event which gave us so much pride in recognition of our pupils' achievements and hard work. Inevitably, time moves on, and taking into consideration commitments to our own children and family, we decided to pause for a while in the full knowledge of the continuing promotion of Irish dancing through the capable hands of our pupils, and in whom we have so much pride.

We thank you all so much, our loyal pupils and parents alike, for the unfailing support you always gave to us, to our own children for your immense contribution in teaching, choreography and organisation. Together we had years of happiness and fun, we will never forget you, we love you all.

Regina Grainger (now Barlow) left, and Maureen Grainger (now Goodwin) on the right. This photograph was taken in 1959 to celebrate Maureen winning and Regina coming second in the Ladies' All-Ireland Dancing Championships. Maureen was the first ever dancer from outside Ireland to win the title. The magnificent trophy is in the centre of the photo together with a good number of other trophies that the sisters had recently won.

The Grainger School of Dancing in the 1950s. Back row, far left, Maureen and Regina Grainger; back row, far right, Brenda Grainger. In the centre with the trophy is Sean Goodwin.

Grainger dancers of the 1960s. Back row, left to right: Josie Melia, Marilyn Rush, Grace Gallagher, Moira Campbell, Kathleen Campbell, Bernadette Keogh. Front row: Ann Cottam, Terence Malone, Thomas Rush, Sean Goodwin, Terence Potter and Collette Glennon.

Photographed at a concert in Houldsworth Hall in the 1960s, here we see Grainger dancers' performance of 'The Aran Islands'. Regina is on piano and Dezi Donnelly Snr is playing the fiddle.

An early photograph of the Grainger School of Dancing. Front row: Regina, Phil, Maureen, Paul and Brenda Grainger. Their mother Regina is pictured fourth from the right on the back row.

Five-year-old Katrina Breslin and six-year-old Kate Donelon at the 2000 Clann na nGael Feis in Didsbury.

Eileen Lally with members of the Lally School of Irish Dancing at a class feis in 1990.

EILEEN LALLY

My dancing career started when I was five years old. My parents took me with my brother and three sisters to Mrs Margaret O'Neal at the Gaelic League which was off St Peter's Square, Manchester. We quickly picked up the steps and were soon winning numerous trophies and medals in Ireland as well as in England. Sadly, Margaret has now died but I will always teach in the same way that she influenced me. As well as learning to dance we took part in Irish language classes and learned to say our prayers in Irish!

When I was eighteen I was asked if I was interested in opening my own school. So, with the help of my sister Rose we decided to give it a go! Our first pupils were our two younger sisters Pat and Kathleen and it wasn't long before we were established as one of the most successful schools in the west. The first pupil from the school to win a major award was Eamonn Lee who became World Champion and All-Ireland Champion at the age of eleven as well as holding many other titles in England and Ireland. Many years later James Keegan also won the world title three times and won every major championship that he competed for including American and European Championships. He is now one of the lead dancers in *Lord of the Dance*. In 1992 we decided to involve more children from just dancing solos and we introduced dance drama, which was now included in the World Championship syllabus. We came second with a story called 'Finnigan's Wake' and followed up the next year by winning with 'Who will marry my daughter?', a comedy which got a standing ovation from the audience.

With the success of *Riverdance*, Irish dancing was in the limelight even more and the classes became more demanding. My niece Claire Usher was now in *Riverdance* with another pupil, Ciara Kennedy, touring America. This is where Claire met her husband Jonathan who was also in the show.

With the sad death of my youngest sister Kathleen in 1996, another of my nieces, Anne Usher, qualified and joined forces with Pat and I to continue the good work. Then another niece qualified, Jane, with Claire and her husband Jonathan, and the classes are the success they are today because of their youth and expertise. We now have another young teacher recently qualified by the name of Megan Healy.

In 2000 I was greatly surprised and honoured to be awarded the MBE by HRH Prince Charles for my services to dancing as well as my work in the Civil Service. That day at Buckingham Palace was indeed one to remember. My adjudicating qualification has taken me all over the world including New Zealand, North America and Canada as well as England, Ireland, Scotland and Wales. If I had not had a career in Irish dancing, I certainly would not have had the chance to see so much of the world. I cannot thank my teacher Margaret O'Neal enough for her encouragement and faith in me. Even this year the school is still winning honours when Jessica Hindley won the All-Ireland Championship and was placed third in the World Championship. Hundreds of children have passed through my classes over the years and many are still in touch to say what wonderful happy times they were. To think I have been teaching Irish dancing for over fifty years and adjudicating for over thirty makes me wonder where all the years have gone. They have been wonderful, happy years and have given me so much to be proud of. To see the children work and play hard is enough reward.

Waiting to dance at the 1990 Qualifying Feis at the UMIST building in Manchester are Ciara Kennedy and Tracy-Anne McMonagle, both with the Lally School of Irish Dancing.

Young dancers of the St Bernadette's School of Dancing in Withington pictured at a ceili in St Bernadette's Hall.

Children of the Lally School of Irish Dancing at their Christmas fancy dress party in the Chorlton Irish Club, 1991.

Young dancers at a Gaelic League function in Manchester in the early 1950s.

In November 2000 the Manchester-based St Wilfrid's branch of Comhaltas Ceoltóirí Éireann celebrated its silver jubilee with a dinner at the Irish World Heritage Centre. Pictured here at the dinner are Labhras O'Murchu Director General of Comhaltas, Eileen Singleton, Pascal Madden, Breege Doherty and Michael Doyle of the St Wilfrid's committee.

Members of the St Wilfrid's branch of Comhaltas Ceoltóirí Éireann at a practice night in 1975. Included here are: the late Mick Levy at the very back (drummer), Philomena McManus, Bernadette Fox, Pat McManus, Seamus Treacey, Caroline Usher, Marie Egan (holding the accordion), Kevin Molloy, Catherine McManus, Kitty Treacey, Frank Featherstone (at the piano), Bill Lennon (to the right of the piano), Kevin Madden (holding fiddle on far right), Margaret Grady, Margaret Gordon, Imelda Gallagher, Susan Rigby, Catherine Flannigan, Chris Cormac sitting on the knee of Marian Flannery, Karen McMullen, Siobhan McMullen (holding accordion), Deidre McManus, Michelle O'Leary.

Young St Wilfrid's traditional musicians pictured in about 1978.

St Wilfrid's junior ceili band playing in 1976.

Traditional music teacher Marian Flannery on left with some of her young protégés in the 1970s.

Young musicians with the O'Carolan branch of Comhaltas at the Northern Regional Fleadh which was held at St Pius School in Rusholme.

Claddagh Step Dancers, captured upstairs in the Irish World Heritage Centre.

Pictured here in 2000 at a regular traditional session at the Jolly Angler pub in the city are Mary Burke, Doug Briggs, Jimmy Barco and Vinnie Short.

At the Northern Regional Fleadh in 1995 are Jemma Farry (aged fourteen) and twelve-year-old Joanne Loftus who won first place in the button accordion competition.

The Northern Regional Fleadh was held in Rochdale in 1996. On the far left is Pat Sweeney, and on the far right is Cllr Rodney Stott, Mayor of Rochdale, with Tara Ceili Band.

Bill Lisgo, Vincent Hyland, Dominic Fitzmaurice, Terry Dowling and Jim O'Connor were all members of the Fianna Phadraig Pipe Band, pictured here at a social night in Wythenshawe in 1991.

At the Clare Music Festival in 1994 10-year-old Adele Farrel won the Father Fullen Cup for the under-12s most promising musician over the weekend. Adele is pictured here with Sean Considine of the Clare Association.

Taking part in the British National Irish Dancing Championships at the Royal College of Music in Manchester in September 1997 are Niamh McKinstry, Senan Fahy and Mary Cox from the Morgan School of Dancing, all ten years old at the time.

Young set dancers representing the 104 Club in Withington about to dance in their first ever competition at the Set Dance Festival held at the Wythenshawe Forum in 1994.

The late, great Wexford man Sean Dempsey in his element set dancing at the English Martyrs Parish Centre. It was thanks to Sean that set dancing became so popular in the Manchester area, and it still is today.

The 104 Club under-10s set dancers taking part in the 2000 Set Dance Festival at the Forum, Wythenshawe.

The patriarch of the Lally dancing dynasty, Jonjo Lally, is pictured here with Colleen McLaughlin (aged five) and James Hackland (four) at a feis in the Chorlton Irish Club, 1990. The young boy in the background is Michael Fox.

ANGELA DURCAN (NÉE USHER)

TRADITIONAL IRISH MUSICIAN, TEACHER AND COMPOSER

Angela Usher, born in Glossop in 1967 to parents Rosemary and Thomas Usher, started learning dancing along with her brothers and sisters from an early age, attending classes at St Kentigern's Primary School on Friday nights and at the English Martyrs Parish Centre on Sunday afternoons. They began performing at local parish events and taking part in competitions with much success. At the age of just seven, Angela qualified for the World Irish Dancing Championships, in the under-11 age group and all five sisters went on the win the North-West Regional Irish Dancing title in their individual age groups. Angela's youngest sister Claire, went on to join *Riverdance*, with which she toured extensively for five years and is an original member of *Riverdance* on Broadway.

The family all attended St Winifred's Primary School, where they were fortunate to benefit from the guidance and great music teaching of Miss Terry Foley. Angela and all her sisters learned to play the guitar with Terry and all the family were involved with St Winifred's school choir, which brought endless hours of enjoyment and performance opportunities.

Towards the end of primary school, Angela and her sister Caroline began taking Irish music lessons. They went along to the Comhaltas Branch of traditional Irish music at St Wilfrid's Social Club in Hulme. The lessons took place on Saturday mornings and Tuesday evenings and Angela started to learn the tin whistle from Marian Egan and Caroline took fiddle lessons with Tony Sullivan and later with Bobby Tracey. Before long, Angela and Caroline were joined by Mark on the tin whistle and flute, Paul began drum lessons with Vinny Levy and Anne took up the tin whistle and piano accordion with Marian.

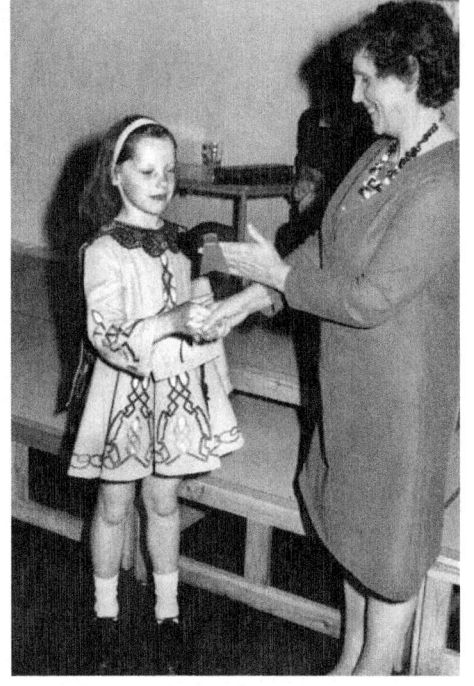

Angela Usher receives a dancing trophy from adjudicator Margaret O'Neal at a feis in the early 1980s.

The family were soon placed in various ceili bands, according to their age group and began competing in Fleadh Cheoils. Angela spent weeks playing a banjo that belonged to Margaret Grady. Margaret showed her the scale and the first few notes of a tune and Angela would sit and work out the rest. Angela also went on to learn the wooden flute from Marian and her mum bought her a wooden flute from the flautist Con Moloney. Angela was also taught the piano, piano accordion and bodhran from Eamonn O'Neal.

The family travelled around the country to take part in the various Fleadh Cheoils. Angela recalls how families would meet at St Bernadette's on Princess Parkway at 4.00 a.m. on a Sunday morning to travel to fleadhs in London and return home at 4.00 a.m. on the Monday morning. The St Wilfrid's 'official' coach driver was Kevin Molloy and he always returned everyone back safe and well. Many of the children who learned their music from Marian Egan, Tony Sullivan, Bobby Tracey and Tony Ryan at St Wilfrid's are still playing music today.

From the age of fourteen, Angela went on to play with the Mayo Youth, which was founded by Michael Forde in Manchester. The group consisted of young musicians from St Wilfrid's, O'Carolan and the Ashton-in-Makerfield Comhaltas branches, along with dancers and singers from around Manchester. There were annual trips to Kiltimagh, County Mayo, as well as a trip to Jersey and numerous performances around Manchester and the UK. Angela started a dance school with Caroline Finn at the Irish Centre in Cheetham Hill and taught there for many years, while also teaching dancing with her aunts and sisters at the Lally School of Irish Dancing. At the same time as she was in the Mayo Youth, Angela also played in a ceili band with Eamonn O'Neal and her brother and sister, Paul and Caroline. After a couple of years the band teamed up with a singing duo from Glossop, to form the Celtic rock band Curragh. Angela played tin whistle and banjo and was joined by Eamonn O'Neal (accordion), Caroline Usher (fiddle), Paul Usher (drums), Martin Coult (guitar and vocals), Sean Wood (lead vocals and bodhran), Mick Coleman (bass guitar) and Terry Foley (vocals). Curragh toured the UK and Ireland until about 1985 and after this, Angela, along with her brother Paul, joined the popular group Toss the Feathers.

From her early teens, Angela taught the guitar and tin whistle to children at her parents' house, but in 1984 Angela was asked to take over the teaching from her sister Caroline at the O'Carolan Branch of Comhaltas, based at St Edward's Parish Hall in Rusholme. Angela quickly began teaching various instruments and putting together ceili bands and Grupa Cheoils for Fleadh Cheoils.

In 1987, the O'Carolan Grupa Cheoil won the age fifteen to eighteen All-Ireland title in Listowel, County Kerry. From 1988, Angela taught at the Tara Branch of Comhaltas, based at the 32 Club in Ardwick Green and the 104 Club in Withington. In 1993, the Tara Grupa Cheoil won the under-twelve All-Ireland title in Clonmel, County Tipperary.

In 1995, Angela put together a Senior Grupa Cheoil with which she played banjo, tin whistle and concertina. This group also went on to win the Senior All-Ireland title in 1995, in Listowel, Co. Kerry. In 1998, Angela then stepped down from teaching with Comhaltas, as she and Peter started their own family. They have four children – Alicia, Grainne, James and Conaill. Their daughters danced for the Lally School of Irish dancing and competed in numerous World Championships, achieving third place in the dance drama at the Glasgow World Championships. The boys both play music, James the guitar and Conaill the bodhran and button accordion.

From 2005, Angela began to teach music in schools around Manchester and now works for One Education Music teaching Irish music and guitar to over 700 children, in Manchester schools, every week. Angela plays socially in Irish music sessions around Manchester and has recently started composing her own tunes, which are now being performed by many musicians. Angela continues to perform with a variety of bands at various gigs and festivals around the UK and Europe.

A 1987 step dance class. Far left is Angela Usher and far right Caroline Finn with some young enthusiastic dancers on the stage at the Irish World Heritage Centre.

Some young members of the Tara branch of Comhaltas back in 1991. Seen here are Sarah and Fidelma Clerkin, Maria Dunleavy, Sabine Stritch, Catherine Campfield, Nuala Murphy, Angela and Claire Usher and Sharon Glendon.

JAMES KEEGAN (LORD OF THE DANCE)

James Felix Keegan was born in September 1986, the youngest of five children to Seamus (of County Leitrim) and Josephine (County Roscommon) Keegan. At the beginning of 1992 James was a member of the Lally School of Irish Dancing and attended his first feis in Blackburn on 6 June 1992 where he was placed first, second and third in all his dances. On 7 March 1993 at a feis in Birmingham, the adjudicator that day, Kathleen Maguire from London, made the unusual step of addressing the crowd before she presented her results. She spoke of how the young boy in the black jacket and cream kilt had performed steps a lot simpler than those he was up against but how he had executed them with style and perfection. 'He was a star of the future,' she said, as she awarded James his first championship. As well as a further nine open championships in the first half of 1994, James became the youngest ever world gold medal holder after taking part in Lally's dance drama *Who will marry my daughter?* James had tasted winning success on the world stage at just seven years of age. On 3 July 1994, he lifted the North American Championship, his first major trophy, with a score of 900 out of 900 points. Two months later, a week after his eighth birthday, he won the British Nationals in Manchester and would win this title a further six times. The Great Britain Championship followed in October and James held the title for eight consecutive years.

In 1995, Mr Tony Hennigan, a teacher at St Bede's College, had formed an Irish music and dance group called Young, Gifted and Green. All the performers, including James, attended the school and the sole purpose of the group was to raise money for charity. Tony Hennigan and his troupe raised over £120,000 for different charities. 1995 also saw James win another North American Major Championship, in Toronto. He flew to the USA and Canada five times between 1994 and 2000 and brought the title home on four occasions. At the end of 1995 James was now old enough to compete in the North-West Qualifying competition for the World Championships the following year. He won his age group and could look forward to competing in the biggest major of them all; however, he didn't win the championship in 1996.

It was 1997 and time for a second attempt at the world title. Again, James finished second. Two months later he won his third North American title in Vancouver followed by wins at the British Nationals and Great Britain Championships later that year. April 1998 was now his third attempt at the world title and this time he finished third. However, on 28 March 1999 in the West County Hotel of Ennis, County Clare, James lifted the world title for the first time at the age of twelve.

The year 2000 would be James' most successful year in competitive Irish dancing. He retained his world title in Belfast as well as every other major possible that year completing a grand slam of Irish dancing majors. He was now All-Ireland, World, North American, British National and Great Britain champion. At the end of 2002, Marie Duffy, choreographer for *Lord of the Dance*, invited James to an audition in London. He finished his final school exam on 12 June 2003 and flew to Nantes, France, on 13 June to join up with troupe 1 of *Lord of the Dance*.

James is now twenty-seven and has been touring with the show for ten years. At the age of seventeen, having been in the show only six months, he was asked to learn the lead role and became the youngest ever lead in the show's history. In 2008 James was awarded a Pride of Eireann Award from the Variety Club for his achievements in Irish dancing. He became a qualified Irish dancing teacher in 2011 and opened the Keegan Academy of Irish Dancing with his sister Louise at the Chorlton Irish Club where he had his first Irish dancing lesson in the same building many years before.

Above, left: James Keegan winning his first dancing trophy at a feis in 1992.
Above, right: Young James Keegan, the new Under-8s National British Champion at the Royal Northen College of Music in 1994. He had recently won the North American Championships in San Diego.

Above, left: James Keegan sitting on the shoulders of Chris Gallagher and Seamus Keegan (his father), 1999. *Above, right:* From one champion to another! James Keegan meets Manchester United manager Sir Alex Ferguson.

5

IRISH WORLD HERITAGE CENTRE & IRISH COMMUNITY CARE (ROSE MORRIS)

Irish World Heritage Centre, 10 Queens Road, Cheetham Hill, Manchester.

The Irish World Heritage Centre in Manchester was officially launched by the Irish Minister for Foreign Affairs, Peter Barry, in 1986. The inspiration for the project came from a group of dedicated Irish people active within the community whose aim was to establish a progressive Irish centre within Manchester where people could meet and socialise. There they would offer a comprehensive programme of activities and events giving visitors and participants unique Irish cultural experiences. It was intended that it would serve as a lasting memorial recognising and acknowledging the contribution made by Irish emigrants across the world down through the centuries and to tell the story of Irish emigration worldwide.

After much searching, the founding members identified a derelict site in Cheetham Hill, which was originally a British Legion Club and beside it the ruins of the Blarney Irish Club, a popular venue, much used by Irish people up until the late 1960s. Both were in need of much renovation. With much volunteer labour on offer and fundraising events held, the work was soon completed. The Irish World Heritage Centre boasted upmarket facilities for the time, with a restaurant, large dance hall, bar and function room and shop. Various classes and clubs were established and to this day there is a busy weekly programme of Irish dance, music, language classes, conferences, evening lectures, educational visits, theatre and live music.

This is the view from the stage when the main hall was under construction.

Wednesday, 1st January, 1986—
THE RANCHERS.

Thursday, 2nd January—
SENIOR CITIZENS' PARTY.

Friday, 3rd January—
AIDEN AND THE STRANGERS.

Saturday, 4th January—
SHILO.

Sunday, 5th January—
Afternoon: DONEGAL ASSOC. CHILDREN'S PARTY.
THE CHAMPIONS; SEAN McSHERRY DISCO.

Friday, 10th January—
IRISH CENTRE FOOTBALL TEAM DANCE; THE BORDERLINE.

Saturday, 11th January—
TOM HEALY AND THE ANTELOPES.

Sunday, 12th January—
Afternoon: DONEGAL ASSOCIATION A.G.M.
COUNTRY BREEZE; SEAN McSHERRY DISCO.

Friday, 17th January—
BALLINGARY REUNION DANCE.

Saturday, 18th January—
SWEENEY BROTHERS & KEVIN FOX; Plus EVERGREEN.

Sunday, 19th January—
LARRY AND THE MOUNTAIN RAMBLERS; SEAN McSHERRY DISCO.

Friday, 24th January—
IRISH CENTRE JUDO CLUB DANCE with FINIAN'S RAINBOW.

Saturday, 25th January—
JOHNNY LOUGHREY AND THE COUNTRYSIDERS.

Sunday, 26th January—
SHILO; SEAN McSHERRY DISCO.

Friday, 31st January—
DONEGAL ASSOCIATION — BORDERLINE SHOWBAND.

FEBRUARY

Saturday, 1st February—
PADDY AND WILD COUNTRY.

Sunday, 2nd February—
BORDERLINE; SEAN McSHERRY DISCO.

****

Monday Nights:
IRISH DANCING

Tuesday Nights:
JUDO CLASSES

Thursday Nights:
MUSIC CLASS Plus PIPE BAND TUITION

An IWHC events schedule from January 1986.

The Irish World Heritage Centre management committee. Terry Mitchell, Matt Maher, Joe McCormack, Brian Kennedy, Pat Feeley, Pat Sweeney, Pat Conway, Jimmy Johnson, Dermot Maguire, Michael Kelly. At the front are Michael Finn and Michael Forde. (Photo by Fox from *Manchester Evening News*)

WORLD LEADERS AND IRISH COUNTY MANAGERS

To mark the special occasion of the opening in 1986, letters of congratulation were received from world leaders of Irish descent and County Managers in Ireland who also sent pictures, craftwork and artefacts connected with each county, many of which are displayed on the walls of the centre.

When opened the centre's crest was an Irish harp but it was changed to the present logo when the name was changed from Irish Centre to Irish World Heritage Centre early in its existence. It is now a bird in flight carrying shamrocks that symbolise exile, freedom and hope as in the flight of Irish people leaving their homes taking their heritage with them to the places where they settled.

PUBLIC MEETING TO ESTABLISH IRISH EDUCATION AND WELFARE ORGANISATIONS, 1984

These organisations were later set up as Manchester Irish Education Group and Irish Community Care. The latter was founded following Fr Emmet Fullen's death when Fr Ahern and Michael Forde secured a grant from the Irish Government to set up an Irish welfare organisation managed separately from St Brendan's and the Irish Centre.

MANCHESTER CEILI AND SET DANCE CLUB

Manchester Ceili and Set Dance Club, founded by the late Sean Dempsey, was first at St Malachy's in Collyhurst but moved to the centre after it opened. The class took place every Monday night and eventually spread to other venues throughout the city. Sean, with John Hennessey, started the annual International Set Dance Festival in 1987 and it still going over 25 years later.

FIRST MANCHESTER IRISH FESTIVAL, 1988

The Irish World Heritage Centre and the Council of Irish Associations were very active at the time with aims to have Irish cultural heritage activities included in Manchester City Council's multicultural programmes. With support from the council they ran a week-long festival in venues across the city which included popular performers such as Míchael Ó Súilleabháin and the Simsa Tire Irish National Folk theatre from Tralee.

FIRST ST PATRICK'S DAY PARADE

The Irish World Heritage Centre held its first St Patrick's Day Parade on 17 March 1990 when the members paraded to St Chad's Church and attended a Mass celebrated by Fr McGarry before returning to the centre. It is interesting to note that at that parade the County Longford Association were the first to display a parade banner.

The following year, 1991, the parade was extended to go to the roundabout at the end of Cheetham Hill Road following Mass in Gaelic at the Irish World Heritage Centre. It was in its third year, 1992, that the St Patrick's Day Parade was extended as far as Albert Square for the first time, where it was reviewed by the Lord Mayor of Manchester, Cllr Billy Egerton.

In March 1993 the parade went again to Manchester Town Hall, but this time it was led by the Lord Mayor of Manchester, Cllr Bill Risby, accompanied by the Mayors of Trafford and Salford. Over the years we have had members of the Irish Government walk with us including Bertie Aherne and ministers Brendan Smith and John O'Donaghue.

Since then we have continued to follow the route from the Irish World Heritage Centre to Manchester Town Hall and back on the return journey for a fun-packed day. It continues to be a major Irish Festival event always preceded by Mass in Gaelic. Fr John Ahern, the well-known Kerry priest, has officiated at nineteen of those Masses and will be officiating for many years to come.

DREAMS OF IRELAND FESTIVAL, 1994

The Aisling Players Drama Group was founded in 1987 and produced Irish plays annually over a 10-year period. Among the dramatic performances staged in that time were *The Playboy of the Western World*, *Juno and the Paycock*, *The Shadow of a Gunman*, *Big Maggie*, *Philadelphia Here I Come*, *Moll*, *The Shaughran*, *The Importance of Being Earnest*, *The Quare Fellow* and the *Beauty Queen of Linane*.

FOUNDATION OF THE MANCHESTER IRISH WRITERS, 1993

The Manchester Irish Writers group was founded in 1993 and has progressed from a small number to a team of twelve very enthusiastic and ambitious writers at various levels in their development. It was founded by Rose Morris and Alrene Hughes in 1993 at the Irish World Heritage Centre. Alrene, assistant head teacher at Woodhey High School, Bury, became and still is the group co-ordinator. She brought to the group her experience of being involved in other writers' groups (ex-Commonword and Bury Writers) and of having had her own stories and poetry and a novel, *Martha's Girls*, published.

Fortnightly meetings are held at the Irish World Heritage Centre and to date they have published five books: *At The End of the Rodden*, a collection of stories and poetry was a long-term aim achieved after two years, and *The Retting Dam* is a collection of poetry launched by Polly Devlin OBE at the 2001 Irish Festival. *Stone of the Heart* was launched in the 2002. In the 2004 Irish Festival two new books were launched: *Kerry Child to Limerick Lady*, the late Ida Kennelly's autobiography edited by her daughter and Manchester Irish Writer, Marion Riley, and *Drawing Breath*, a collection of monologues first performed by the writers in the Royal Exchange Theatre in September 2003. They set up their own publishing company called Scribhneoiri (the Gaelic word for writers).

Manchester Irish Writers Group, 1997.

DREAMS OF IRELAND FESTIVAL, 1994

The Irish World Heritage Centre held a week-long drama festival as their input to Manchester City's Year of Drama in 1994. It was officially opened by the Lord Mayor of Manchester, Cllr Sheila Smith who really enjoyed watching Nuala Bradwell's interpretation of *Moll*, which was staged to a full house on three nights. There was a night of entertainment around the fireside with actress Margaret Nyland from County Mayo as Bean a Tí and a performance in the Gaelic language called *Blas Beirte* by Aine Moynihan from Dingle with musical accompaniment by her daughter Muireann Nic Amhlaoibh who is now a well-known member of Danú.

Mike Harding was host for a night with storytelling and poetry with support from St Wilfrid's musicians who have used the centre as their base since St Wilfrid's Parish Hall in Hulme closed down. Multi-award winning Michelle O'Leary from the group is carrying on the good work started by Pascal and Nora Madden and Seamus and Kitty Tracey almost forty years ago. Everyone attending concerts around Britain and Ireland will have heard Nora and Kitty lilting as only they can.

Performers at the Dreams of Ireland Festival held as part of Manchester's Year of Drama, 1994. Here we see Muireann Nic Amhlaoibh from Dingle, singer and musician and now a member of Danú; Margaret Breen; Mike Harding; Michael McNally; actress Geraldine Boucher and Aine Moynihan, Muireann's mother, following their performance in the Gaelic language drama, *Blas Beirte*.

Michael D. Higgins visited the IWHC in 1994 as Minister of Arts and Culture and is seen here with John Keane, President of the IWHC.

At the front door of the Irish World Heritage Centre in 2000, on the day which Irish Minister Seamus Brennan came to present the £1million Millennium Grant for the new Irish Diaspora Museum. Left to right: Cllr Pat Karney, Cllr Martin Pagel (the Lord Mayor of Manchester), Cllr Tony Byrne, hidden behind him is Mark Howard (manager of the IWHC), -?-, Tom Burke (management committee), Irish Minister Seamus Brennan, Paddy Geoghegan (management committee), Cllr Kath Robinson, Danny Greer (management committee), Tom Ely (management committee), Michael Forde (Chair of the IWHC), Pascal Madden (management committee).

CONRADH NA GAELIGE

Emmet Fullen Branch of Conradh na Gaelige has been holding weekly language classes for over 20 years. One of its founder members, the late Liam McLoughlin, was a very active and dedicated member of the management committee and participated in all things connected with Irish heritage and culture during that time.

VISITORS TO THE IRISH WORLD HERITAGE CENTRE

Since it was established, the centre has had visitors from all over the world. Official visits were made by Presidents Mary Robinson and Mary McAleese; Taoiseachs Albert Reynolds and John Bruton and Bertie Ahern and British Prime Ministers Tony Blair and Gordon Brown. In addition to these there have been countless other distinguished visitors including Peter Barry, Michael D. Higgins, Sile de Valera, Noel Dempsey, Dermot Aherne, Brendan Smith, John O'Donahue, Mary Harney, Enda Kenny, Seamus Brennan, Mary O'Rourke and Michael O'Kennedy.

The American Ambassador to Ireland, Jean Kennedy Smith, was a visitor in 1997. On other occasions Cardinal Hume, John Hulme and Gerry Kelly have all visited. Mo Mowlam visited the centre on three occasions, once with Liz Dawn (Vera Duckworth from *Coronation Street*), while many sporting personalities have dropped in, including Jack Charlton, Kevin Moran, Barry McGuigan, Alex Higgins, Shay Given and Stephen Roche.

Michael Maher and Dermot Maguire (secretary, IWHC management committee), meeting Taoiseach Bertie Ahern.

President Mary Robinson and Tom Burke, 1996.

THE NEW IRISH WORLD HERITAGE CENTRE

We are now in the transition of moving from the old Irish World Heritage Centre to our brand new premises just 200 metres further along Queens Road. It has been designed to follow the curve of an ancient Irish Fort. It will be glass- and stone-fronted with views through the building, out into the garden area set against the backdrop of our Manchester skyline. We are in partnership with Manchester City Council in delivering this project and enjoy total support from the Irish Government. We are in negotiations regarding a Metro stop at the new centre which will be named Irish Town. The new centre will not only improve on the facilities that we had to offer in the past for the Irish and wider communities, but it will be one of the premier visitor attractions of the city with a museum dedicated to the story of the Irish diaspora worldwide.

There is hardly a country in the world that has not felt the benefit of the positive contribution made by Irish emigrants. Men and women who left Ireland over the centuries have become educators, entrepreneurs, entertainers, political leaders and heads of state in many foreign countries. Throughout the world their cultural legacies endure and the Irish World Heritage Centre is dedicated to keeping alive the memory and achievements of these people. It is a celebration of their success and their major contribution to world progress and a continuity of Ireland's story embracing the Irish global family of 70 million people. Their vision statement says:

> Our vision is the establishment of a centre of excellence outside of Ireland that will provide unique visitor facilities, exhibitions, entertainment, sport and accommodation delivered by advanced multimedia and information technology media. Phase one will house a theatre, community room, shop and education suite, while phase two will see the construction of a conference centre, health centre, playing fields, restaurant and museum.

The Taoiseach visits the IWHC in February 2009. Left to right: Cllr Naeem Hassan, -?-, Bertie Ahern, Cllr Maryam Khan, her father Cllr Afzal Khan, Cllr Pat Karney and Michael Ford, Chairman of the IWHC.

THE IRISH DIASPORA FOUNDATION

Following the Irish Government Millenium Award, the Irish Diaspora Foundation, a registered charity, was set up in 2002 by the Irish World Heritage Centre to be governed by a board of trustees to work on plans for the new development. Its aims and objectives are to advance the education of the wider community and the promotion and development of Irish arts, history, cultural heritage and sporting activities, to establish an Irish Diaspora Museum and to work in partnership with other Irish organisations and community groups.

In 2004 the Irish Diaspora Foundation secured funding from the Heritage Lottery Fund, Dion (Irish Government), enabling the employment of two full time staff members, based at the Irish World Heritage Centre , Margot Ryan, in Education and Cultural Development and John O'Rourke, Administrative Technician and Graphic Designer. We are also assisted in the work by a number of willing and committed volunteers.

IRISH DIASPORA MUSEUM

The Irish Diaspora Museum will celebrate the positive contribution made by the Irish worldwide. Collections, documents and exhibitions will present the history of Irish emigration and the development of the global Irish family. The collections are broad in scope, ranging from fine and decorative arts to Irish social, domestic and industrial history. Artefacts from five continents will be displayed around the new centre so the entire building becomes an expression of Irish history, heritage and culture from around the world.

THE FOUNDATION OF IRISH COMMUNITY CARE IN MANCHESTER, FR JOHN AHERN

Naturally I have an affinity with all things Irish. I was aware of the problems of the Irish as an ethnic minority – not all would have seen things in that light but in the 1980s other ethnic minorities were making their presence felt and we also needed a voice at the Manchester City Council Committee for Community Relations. I was always interested in things cultural, in the language, music, dance, and the folklore of Ireland.

On Fr Emmett Fullen's untimely death in 1985, Bishop Kelly asked me to stay on in Salford for a year as parish priest of St Lawrence's and to run St Brendan's Irish Centre. My first duty was the funeral of Fr Emmett and it was at his wake that Orla O'Halloran from the Irish Embassy came to me and said there was money available for emigrant projects in Great Britain. The fund was to be known as Dion (Gaelic for roof) and St Brendan's, because of Fr Emmett's work, was earmarked to receive a grant from this fund. I declined the offer asking if I could first speak with Irish groups in the city. Not all were in favour of what I proposed. Michael Forde, chairperson of the newly opened Irish Centre in Cheetham Hill, was very keen so we decided to have an organisation that would be independent of all Irish centres and organisations but would be supported by them and they would be represented on the management committee. I went to the Cross and Passion Congregation where I knew Sister Patricia, the Provincial, as we had worked together in Peru. I asked if they could help. She told me I was dead lucky as one of their sisters had just returned from Peru and if willing she could take up an appointment in the project. That is how Sister Rosaleen Murray another veteran of Villa el Salvador became our first director. Another friend, Fr Bobby Gilmore from the Irish Chaplaincy in London, was of immense help in setting the project up as a registered charity and giving us a constitution.

Fr Emmett was a one-man Community Care. He had great people around him who helped out, people from the Saint Vincent de Paul Society and the Legion of Mary . . . I think of people like Joe Moran, the late Harry Purcell, Tommy Duffy, the late Kathleen Donnelly and Ita Mulligan. The late Noreen Finn was another stalwart of that era. There were so many around St Brendan's in those days and they were forerunners of today's Irish Community Care volunteers but they did not have an organisation – nothing formal was in existence. You could say ICC grew out of Fr Emmett's grave. Just over a quarter of a century later it is still going from strength to strength – what a fitting tribute to the life and work of a man from Desertmartin.

The 1991 management committee. Sean Reynolds, Michael Forde, Tommy McKenna, Pat McKnight, Majella Dunne, Sister Elizabeth Cahill, Noreen Finn, Anne Hilferty at an ICC management committee meeting in 1991 following the opening of the Cheetham Hill premises that year.

Seen here with the Irish Community Care banner are Sheila O'Regan, Joe Flynn (Chair of Manchester Irish Education Group), Margaret Molloy (volunteer ICC), Michael Cassidy (management committee of ICC, Phil Moffat, Tommy Foley (volunteer ICC) and Walter Cassin (volunteer ICC).

Joe and Margaret McCormack, Noreen Finn, Sister Rosaleen Murray, Mary Forde and Mr and Mrs McCabe, attending one of the early ICC fundraising dances at the IWHC in 1988.

IRISH COMMUNITY CARE, ST LAWRENCE'S, OLD TRAFFORD

Sister Rosaleen Murray CP was the first manager of Irish Community Care. The organisation was registered as a charity and it had three aims and objectives when started up in 1985 using the parish offices at St Lawrence's, Old Trafford, as its base:

> To relieve the effects of old age, poverty, sickness and distress
>
> To provide facilities in the interest of social welfare for recreation and leisure time occupation with the object of improving the conditions of life for the said people.
>
> To provide for the burial of people with no next of kin.

There has never been any reason to change them as they covered every aspect of the work intended to done and are still as relevant today as they were then.

The Irish Community Care emblem, chosen by Sister Rosaleen in 1985, is the St Bridget's Cross and the organisation's motto is 'Together we serve'. When Sister Rosaleen left in 1989 she was followed by another member of the Cross and Passion order, Sister Elizabeth Cahill, who was manager from that time until April 2002. During those years there was a lot of expansion and development to meet the ever-increasing needs within the Irish and wider community.

Tommy Whelehan (the manager of the IWHC), Noreen Finn (ICC Trustee and Treasurer), Bass representative and Sister Elizabeth Cahill at the presentation of a cheque for funds raised by the Bass Brewery.

IRISH COMMUNITY CARE AT CHEETHAM HILL ROAD

Irish Community Care moved to the house at 289 Cheetham Hill Road, its current head office, which was officially opened by Bertie Ahern, then Irish Government Minister for Labour, in February 1991. The renovation of these premises was made possible by a generous grant of £58,000 from Manchester City Council in 1989. On the same day as the opening ceremony, the Irish Abroad Charitable Trust presented Irish Community Care with a new minibus.

The first volunteer meeting at the new ICC house in Cheetham Hill in 1991. Back row, left to right: Lilly Dilger, Mary Forde, Peggy O'Connor, Bernadette Merrigan, Anne Groarkin, Sister Elizabeth Cahill, Kath Walsh. Front row, seated: Emby Walsh, Nora Higgins, Rose Morris, Noreen Finn, Majella Dunne, Phil Moffat. Seated on floor: Mary Keenan and Rose Clements.

FUNDRAISING WITHIN THE IRISH AND WIDER COMMUNITY

1999 Sister Elizabeth and friends on a sponsored walk in Heaton Park.

ICC volunteers and staff at the Grove. On the back row are Kath Cunningham, Deirdre Carroll, Sister Brenda Dorrian, Mary Somers, Alice Egan, Sarah Butcher, Mary Gallogly, Michael Cassidy. Among the front row: Steve Beckett, Jimmy Cunningham, Sister Elizabeth Cahill, Nora Higgins.

IRISH COMMUNITY CARE EXTENDS ITS SERVICES TO LEVENSHULME

The official opening of an Irish Community Care office on Stockport Road was carried out by Mary Harney, Irish Minister for Enterprise, Trade and Employment, in 1998. Following regeneration on the A6 it was necessary to move from that premises to one near to Elbow Street. This was officially opened by the Irish Ambassador, Dáithí Ó Ceallaigh in January 2004.

Tommy McKenna (chairman), Dáithí Ó Ceallaigh (the Irish Ambassador), Sharon Naughton (former Lady Mayoress of Salford), Michael Coen, Deirdre Carroll, Antoinette Ó Ceallaigh, Mary Johnson and Monica Sloyan at the official opening of the ICC Levenshulme office in 2004.

The initial financial support for Irish Community Care came from the Irish Government Dion Fund in 1985. That funding continued and increased as new projects were established and is still funding a major part of the operations of Irish Community Care, providing the salaries for the manager, a number of staff and the Graves project. It is now known as the Emigrant Support Programme within the Department of Foreign Affairs.

As with all organisations there are substantial overheads and administration and for this Irish Community Care relies on Irish and wider community fundraising events and donations. Some projects are supported by Manchester, Salford and Trafford local government grants and partnerships and Irish Community Care have also benefited from Heritage Lottery and Children in Need funds for the salaries of project workers.

OVER-FIFTIES SOCIALS AND CRAFT GROUPS

The first monthly senior citizens' social was held on Sunday 29 June 1987 at St Lawrence's parish centre. It later moved to the Irish World Heritage Centre where it is still in existence but now it is held weekly, on a Wednesday, currently looked after by volunteer coordinator Katherine Cunningham and twenty-five very willing volunteers with an average attendance of 150. In addition, over the years weekly socials for the over-fifties were set up across the city, in the Grove and later St Richard's, Longsight, St Anne's, Old Trafford, a men's group in the Sacred Heart, Gorton and craft groups in St Mary's, Levenshulme and in Salford at Chetwood Community Centre, Marlborough Road School and the Hub. All of these are made possible by the major input of a very dedicated group of hardworking volunteers.

Mary's Craft Group, 2002. Among this talented group are Alice Egan, Mary Tonner, Jean Devanny, Agnes Lynch, Sally Lanagan, Mary Ashe, Nora Doherty, Doris O'Keefe, Mary Hamilton, Mary Houlihan, Maude Deay, Irene Rowlands, Teresa Shaw, Anne McDowell, Sister Elizabeth Cahill, Marjorie Hoey, Christine Mooney, Marie McNeill. At the front are Joyce Kaye, Anne Bradbury, Kath Cunningham, Sister Brenda Dorrian, Evelyn Keogh.

Della Costello, Kath Cunningham, Mary Somers and Alice Egan at volunteers' dinner at the IWHC. Volunteers have an annual dinner celebration each February on the weekend nearest to St Bridget's feast day.

IRISH COMMUNITY CARE MINIBUS

There is always a great demand for the minibus for transport to events and it was a much appreciated gesture by Cllr Jim King, Mayor of Salford, in 2003, when he nominated Irish Community Care as the charity to which he wished the mayoral fund for his year in office to be donated for the purchase of a new minibus to replace the one that had been donated in 1991 by the Irish Abroad Charitable Trust.

This minibus in turn was replaced in 2012 following a one-year fundraising campaign by Tommy McKenna, Chairman of Irish Community Care, in which he was supported by contractors, businesses and members of the Irish and wider community in raising the £45,000 necessary to put this minibus on the road.

The first new minibus – Olive Hogan and friends going on a trip.

THE FORGOTTEN IRISH AND BURIALS OF THOSE WITH NO NEXT OF KIN

The first grave was acquired in 1986. That grave was used up until 1994 after twelve burials had taken place. Members of the Irish community donated other graves to ICC in Southern Cemetery and in Gorton.

Before Irish Community Care's foundation many of the active County Associations would have made an effort to deal with the funeral of a fellow county member who had no next of kin, who had lost touch, or severed relations with their family in Ireland. They continue to be very supportive of this project especially in fundraising.

Deirdre Carroll, who retired from the manager's position last year, took a special interest in this project during her many years in Irish Community Care, setting up a system of good working contacts with the police and coroner's office so that those Irish found dead with no next of kin would be referred for funeral arrangements and burial. Sometimes with a little bit of local knowledge and research those referred can have relatives discovered who are keen to continue with a family funeral or even have the remains taken back for burial in Ireland. Again the relatives are helped along the way with this process should they require.

Volunteers participating in a workshop on annual review day. Jim Molloy, Nan Cummins, traveller families project coordinator Margaret Cowen, Jean Devanny, Mary Somers, Nora Higgins, Michael Cassidy.

ROSE MORRIS

Rose Morris was born in Altaglushan, near Dungannon in County Tyrone. After graduating in Art and Design at Belfast College of Art and gaining her Art Teacher's Diploma at Birmingham University, she settled in Manchester with her husband, John, and two sons.

In Manchester she has had a long involvement as a volunteer within the Irish community – she has been a member of the management committee of the Irish World Heritage Centre since 1987 where she serves as their cultural officer. Rose is also a trustee and arts and culture director of the Irish Diaspora Foundation involved with the development of the new Irish World Heritage Centre.

Rose has initiated and coordinated many Irish cultural and cross-community programmes. Retired from a thirty-year career in art and design education in Greater Manchester schools and colleges, she has extensive knowledge of the Irish arts, literature, and heritage, which she pursued through cultural activities, international festivals and educational exchange programmes which included the EU Celtic Peoples' Project and East West educational initiative of the Good Friday Agreement.

She has made extensive use of her interests and skills as a published writer and poet, artist and photographer in promotional initiatives and events on the cultural programmes of the Irish World Heritage Centre, the Irish Diaspora Foundation and the Manchester Irish Festival.

She also serves on the committees of the Manchester Irish Festival and the Manchester Irish Writers, which she co-founded, and in the past has been an active committee member of the Aisling Players, the Irish Professional Network and the Tyrone Association.

ICC received the Investors in People Award in 2002. Back row: Rachel Lynch, Steve Beckett, Chris Murray, Martin Naughton, Timothy Bradley, Mary Johnson and Sister Nuala O'Connor. Front row: Robin Bailey, Rose Morris, Deirdre Carroll, Anne Rabbitt.

President Mary McAleese meets the Irish Community Care Management Committee. Michael Cassidy, Pat Sweeney, Pat Cassidy, Fr John Ahern, Tommy McKenna, President Mary McAleese, Nancy Ely, Rose Morris and Sister Elizabeth Cahill. (*Photo by Bob Anderson*)

6

IRISH COUNTY ASSOCIATIONS (MANCHESTER)

Pictured here are the folk who met up at the inaugural meeting of the Manchester Sligo Association in December 1984.

Donegal Association Committee and friends at the annual dinner in the Manor Hey Hotel in 1984.

Clare Association dinner at the Britannia Ringway Hotel in 1990. Seated: Margaret Sheehy, Teresa Coughlan, Breege Crosse, Claire Finn. Standing: Tommie Moore, Pat Mooney and John Fahey.

Kildare folk at the Kildare Association's first ever dance, held at the Grove Club in October 1993.

In April 1993 the Manchester Offaly folk held an inaugural meeting at the Crown pub to set up a new Manchester Offaly Association. Pictured here are Sean Reilly, Michael Hannon, Teresa Leonard, Sean Kelly and Kay Lynam.

The Wexford Association's annual dinner was held at the Irish World Heritage Centre in 1991.

Members of the Roscommon Association Committee at their annual dinner in 1993.

Enjoying a Kildare Association function in 1993 are Tommie Roche, Anne Marie Breheny, Lisa Whelan, Tom Hughes, Angela Whelan and Ann Hughes.

Carlow dinner at the Irish World Heritage Centre in 1996. Seen here are Marcella Geoghegan, Mary Condron, Jim Cuddy and Paddy Geoghegan who was chairman and founder of the association.

Three of the founder members of the Cavan Association: John and Anne Lynch and John McManus, photographed at the 1998 annual dinner at the Grove.

In June 1995 the Down Association held its first dance at the English Martyrs Parish Centre. Pictured here are members of the first committee, Tom Lambe (PRO), Charlie Bailey (secretary), P.J. Morgan (chairman), Ann Bailey (treasurer) and Brian Ahern (assistant PRO).

Pictured at a Meath Association dance at St Kentigern's Club in 1995 are Martin and Anne Crilly, Bridget Keenan, Kathleen O'Connor, Simon Walsh and Larry Keenan.

Meeting at a Leitrim Association dance in St Kentigern's Club in 1996 are Josie Heeran; Sarah Griffin; Elizabeth Fereday and Siobhan, Claire and Deirdre Griffin.

Galway Association Dinner, 2000. John and Una Madden with Mary and Tommie Kelly at the Irish World Heritage Centre.

The Tyrone Association annual dinner at the Irish World Heritage Centre in 1998. Pictured here are Rose Morris (secretary of the association), Tyrone footballers Cormac McAnallen and Enda McGinley with the Tom Markham Cup which they helped to win when they won the All-Ireland Minor Championship, and association chairman Peter O'Neill.

At the Kilkenny dinner in 1999 at the Lancashire County Cricket Club are association stalwarts Pat, Jimmy and Martin O'Shea.

Nobel Peace Prize winner John Hulme was the guest speaker at the 1996 Annual Mayo Association dinner at Old Trafford, pictured here with Frank and Marcella Wilkinson of the Manchester Mayo Association.

Founder members of the Manchester Wicklow Association pictured at their annual dinner at the Grove Club in 1994. Here are Billy and Chris Dunne and Bernadette and Peter Merrigan.

Dublin Association dinner at the Irish World Heritage Centre in 1998. Back row: Tom Doyle, Chris, Michelle and Tony Flynn. Front row: Teresa Flynn and Sue Doyle.

Louth Association dance at the Grove in 1996. Standing are Jimmy and Andy Murphy. Seated, John, Angela and Lucy Murphy.

In July 1990 the Roscommon Association held a competition at the 32 Club to choose a girl to represent the Manchester association at the Roscommon Rose final later that summer. The girl chosen to represent Manchester was Anne-Marie Keenan who is pictured here with the other entrants in the competition. Philomena Collins, Anne-Marie Keenan (winner), Yvonne Mitchell, Diane Smith, Michelle Carney.

Tipperary Association dinner at the Irish World Heritage Centre in February 1995. John Wilson, Sharon, Jimmy and Noreen Pollard, John and Maria Connor.

Friends of the Meath Association celebrate at the Irish World Heritage Centre, 1980s.

7

ST ANN'S GAA (STRETFORD) 1999–2009

Fr John Ahern with Kerry sporting heroes and the Sam Maguire Cup on the pitch at Old Trafford, home of Manchester United – Aidan O'Mahony (star defender), Jack O'Connor (trainer), Gerh O' Keefe (selector) and Owen Rochford, Manchester United's no. 1 supporter.

HISTORY COMPILED BY JOHN KELLY

The first documented evidence of St Ann's GAA is to be found in the minutes from a county board meeting held at the Irish Centre, Liverpool, on Saturday 1 May 1965. It referred to them taking part in the Wolfe Tone Cup where they beat Eire Og by 1–1 pts to 0–0 pts. Unfortunately no other reports were recorded in the history books on the progress of St Ann's GAA in this competition for that year and there are no records of the club having any success in those early days of its existence. Sadly, there are no records of the club's existence after 1968.

Within the county at that time, there were eleven Gaelic football clubs and seven hurling clubs. Fr Emmet Dagens played a major role in the club during those early days and indeed was one of the original founder members of the club. Other names associated with the club in the early days are P. Kavanagh, W. Hayes, S. Mahon, M. Ryan, T. Lyons and M. Gaule.

In a telephone conversation with John Kelly on 9 May 2009, Fr Dagens related that the first ever football kits and footballs used by the club were donated by their neighbours Manchester United. Fr Dagens' contact with Manchester United was with the famous goalkeeper Pat Dunne, who approached United on behalf of Fr Dagens with a view to sponsoring their kit; a request which they duly and kindly obliged. In the same conversation with John, Fr Dagens also stated that on one occasion Pat Dunne played in a game of football for St Ann's and that he also persuaded the United team to come out and watch games of hurling on a Sunday afternoon.

Fr Dagens was a priest at St Ann's from 1960 to 1967. He was then appointed to a parish in Bury but he still kept his involvement with the club. In 1969 he was then transferred to Ireland. Fr Dagens was a prominent member at County Board level: being elected as president of the association on 23 January 1966 at the annual general meeting in Liverpool and re-elected to the post in 1967 and 1968.

He was also responsible for securing a full-size pitch at Turn Moss from Stretford Corporation for a fee of 30s per game, as recorded in the minutes of the county board meeting dated 2 July 1967. Fr Dagens is still involved with the local club team in Newry and now resides in the little village of Kilcoo, 8 miles south of Newry, County Down. To the best of our knowledge, and after many enquiries, we think these are the whereabouts of some of the founder members of the club: Peter Kavanagh returned to Ireland to join the Garda Siochana and is now retired; Tommy Lyons passed away but used to live in Altrincham and as for Bill 'Willie' Hayes, S. Mahon, M. Gaule and R. Ryan, we have no records of their whereabouts since 1968.

The club was re-formed at a meeting held on 4 November 1999. The new founding members were Danny Grogan, Colm Coyne, and Pat Frainey. Also at the meeting, the following officers were elected for the forthcoming year.

Chairman:	Colm Coyne
Vice Chairman:	Danny Grogan
President:	Monsignor Arthur Keegan
Vice President:	Pat Grady
Secretary:	Kevin Archer
Assistant Secretary:	Margaret Ahern
Treasurer:	Gerry Murray
Assistant Treasurer	Alex Hunt

Initially, St Ann's GAA was founded as an under-age club to promote our national game of Gaelic Football within the Irish community of Stretford. This area has always had a large Irish population and many of the second-generation Irish live here and in the surrounding districts. Danny Grogan was the figurehead from the outset, with his ability to coach boys to play the game. He could see that there was a need to form a club in Stretford and one day, during a conversation, he wondered if there was any way that we could achieve this. Danny had a wealth of talented young lads that he was coaching and he felt that a Stretford club would benefit from this as he had boys from the parish playing for another club within the county. Another reason for this was because he did not want to lose the boys permanently to another club.

In order for this to go ahead we approached Monsignor Keegan, the parish priest of St Ann's Church, Stretford, with the idea and for his approval. He had no objection to this and became our club chaplain as well as being chaplain to Manchester United.

Colm Coyne and Danny Grogan approached the county board at their meeting on 12 July 1999 with a proposal of forming an underage GAA club at St Ann's in Stretford. A discussion with the county board and delegates took place, the outcome being that they felt this was a good idea but they raised the query that it would be detrimental to the other under-age clubs in the county, as most of the players to be used by St Ann's were registered with them. However, the board gave the go-ahead to Colm and Danny.

Our thanks must go to Tommy Green of Green Plant Hire who donated and sponsored the first kit. The colours and crest for it were taken from St Ann's School, which we are proud to represent. Today, St Ann's GAA club is based at the St Ann's Social Club, which is the former St Ann's Roman Catholic School in Stretford. This is still where we continue to have our meetings and our fundraising functions. The club is now well and truly established in the community.

The 2004 under-12s team. Seen here are John Kildunne, Kieran Gaughan, Liam Kildunne, Sam McCauley, Patrick Walsh, Jack Huxley and, on the front row, Ashley Mercer, Marcus Paradiuk, Joseph Niland, David Ford, Declan Lyons and Daniel Bannister.

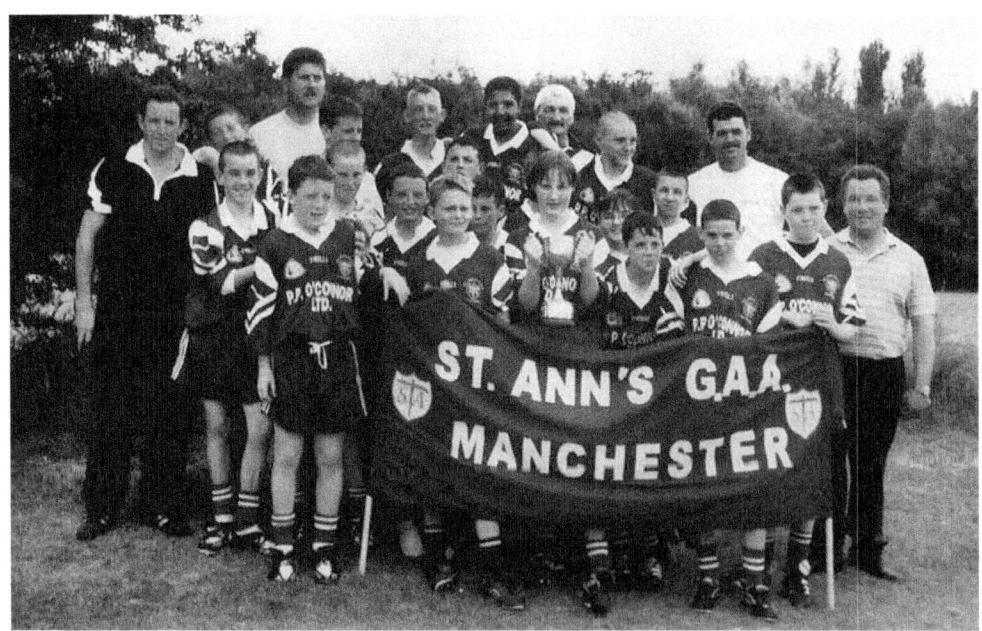

The under-14s All Britain Trophy Winners in 2000. Seen here are Danny Grogan, Pat Frainey, Colm Coyne, John Kelly, Pat Grady, Willie Ahern, Michael Grogan, Michael and Martin Gallagher, Jack Coleman, Liam Coyne, Jonathan Kelly, Ryan Brown, Johnny Reddin and Siobhan Murphy. Captain Katie Mellet is at the front holding the cup.

Shirt sponsors Peter O'Connor and Tommy Halligan with Colm Coyne.

The 2004 All Britain Junior final team.

A ticket for the first ever annual dinner dance at Lancashire County Cricket Club, Friday 22 October 2004.

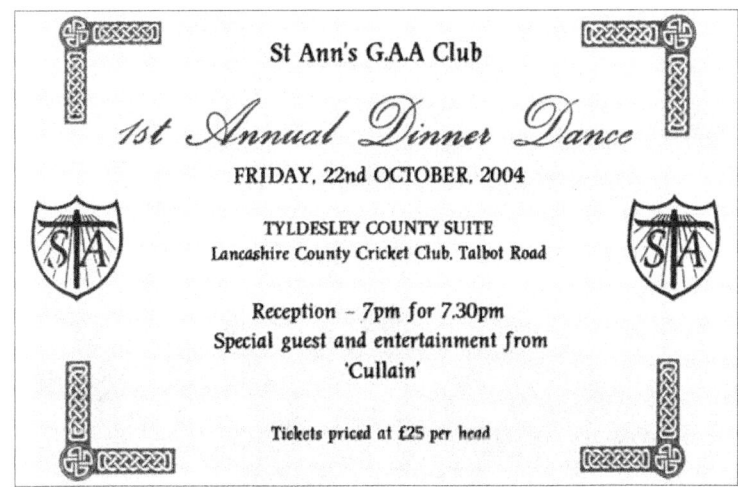

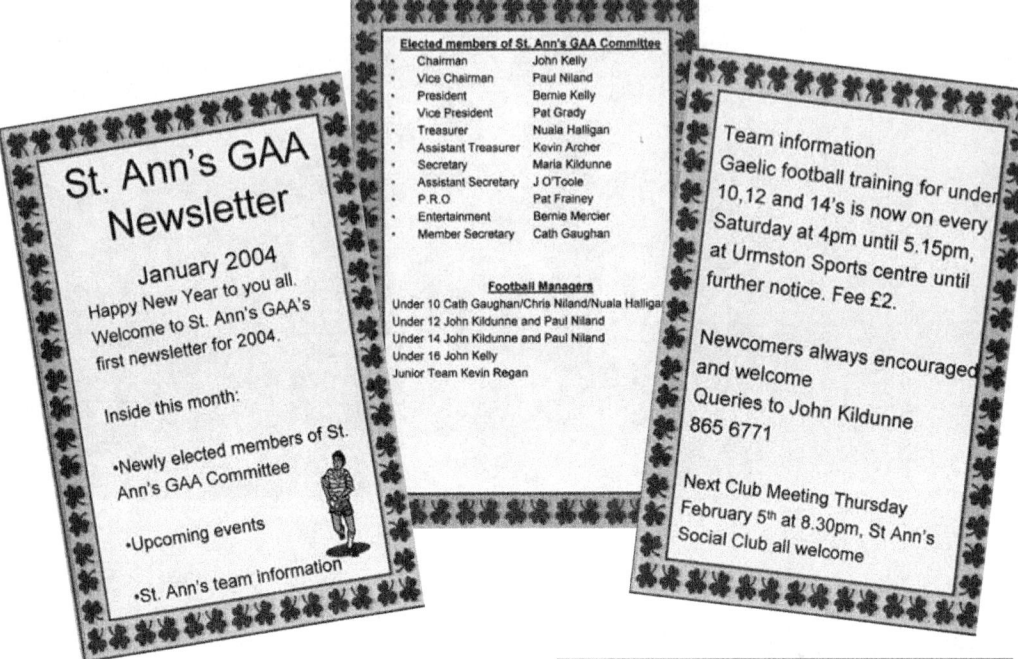

The first St Ann's newsletter, 2004.

A sporting event with Michael O'Muircheartaigh (the voice of the Gaelic Games) in 2006.

Celebrating at St Ann's Social Club; Colm Coyne, Danny Grogan, Peter O'Connor, John Hogan, Sean Walsh, Thomas Grady, Michael Grogan, Jonathan Kelly, Ben Sullivan, Mick Higgins, Jonathan Reddin, Liam Coyne, Paul Walsh, Richard Deloughrey, Willie Ahern, Mark and Michael Davitt, John Fitzpatrick, Mark Mulgrave and Chris Keating.

Seen here at Lancashire County Cricket club are Pat Frainey, Gerard Henry, TV & radio presenter Eamon O'Neal, Toby McWalter and Pat Fallon (All-Star Mayo Footballer).

Here we see Fr John Ahern, John Kelly, Derek Savage (Galway senior Footballer), Bernadette Kelly, Fr Pat Greasley and Danny Grogan.

Peter O'Connor, Danny McGrath, Tommy Halligan, Dave Parker, Peter Quinn and Dermot McKenna.

Chris Ford, Paul Walsh, -?-, Joe Walsh, Tom Hennigan, Ted Grogan, John Walsh and Vinnie Duffy.

MEMORIES OF ST ANN'S GFC, STRETFORD, PAT FRAINEY

I arrived in Manchester in 1976. I wanted to see for myself what the work situation was like as things were quiet in the west of Ireland. There was always plenty of work as I was brought up on a farm but not a lot of money about. Leaving home (County Mayo) was not easy; apart from my close family, I also left behind some lovely people at Carrmore/Hollymount Football Club where I played at under-age level, from under-12 to under-16.

During the first years In Manchester I heard of St Brendan's GFC where I played a few games in the late 1970s. When out on a night out I met up with John Kelly and some other players who played with Oisin GFC. A few beers and a few hours later, I became an Oisin player and the next day John thanked me for making such a big decision in the middle of the night . . . and he's been buying the beer ever since.

I made many friends over the years through my association with Gaelic football in Lancashire and Oisin GFC. When injury cut short my playing career it was difficult to watch from the sidelines, so when Danny Grogan called by my house with Colm Coyne to discuss the setting up of St Ann's GFC, I was only too delighted to help.

With fewer players around, setting up a new GAA club in Lancashire in the late 1990s was not going to be easy. Great credit goes to Danny Grogan as it was his idea that we should set up St Ann's GFC (under-age) and Danny was always involved in the coaching of under-age players and had the support of their parents to sign for St Ann's Club.

My initial thought was who can I call on for support? Well one man in particular I would like to mention is Joe Cahill (Kildare & Oisin GFC) for all his help. Also Mike Cunningham for arranging and looking after the football pitch at Turn Moss (St Ann's Home Ground), Dave Parker for providing the very first trophies to the club, Jimmy Gallagher (Goat Tavern pub, Claremorris, County Mayo) and the late Gerard Henry (Claremorris, County Mayo).

St Ann's GFC started out with three under-age teams – under-10, under-12 and under-14 – and with lots of interest the club started a junior team. It was the under-14 team, though, that was going to create history at Turn Moss. On 23 July 2000 they clinched their first provincial title at their very first attempt. They would have to overcome strong opposition from teams from Oxford and Cardiff before they defeated Sean McDermott's highly rated team from Warwickshire in the provincial under-14 Club Championship football final in emphatic style, and came out worthy winners by 4–5 to 0–0. The team coach and selectors were Danny Grogan, Padraig Frainey and Pat Grady.

Our under-10 and under-12 sides had a good first year playing some outstanding football at the annual tournament held at Turn Moss on 28 May 2000, and what a successful tournament it turned out to be, with teams from Leeds and Cardiff taking part. St Ann's under-12 team had an impressive victory over St Colmcilles of Cardiff – St Ann's 2–4 St Colmcilles 2–1.

The junior team got off to a slow start but now with nearly twenty players from between 14 and 18 years of age and coached by Colm Coyne, the future looks bright.

Seen here are some of the ladies from St Ann's GAA at their presentation evening; Maria Kildunne, Stephanie Callaghan, Rachel Hogan, Caroline McKenna, Becky Hogan, Ciara Frainey, Siobhan Murphy, Alice Galvin, Carol Lavin, Lisa Grady, Caroline Mannion, Orla Mannion, Lisa Brehon and Kathryn Galvin.

St Ann's under-14s team in 2004. Paul Niland, Ciaran Hopkins, Sean and Ciaran Gaughan, Thomas Halligan, Joseph Niland, Liam Kildunne, Tom Murdoch, Martin Worth and John Kildunne.

John Kildunne, Julie Kildunne, Liam Kildunne, Maria Kildunne, Paul Kildunne, Julia Kildunne and John Kildunne Snr are seen here at the St Ann's annual dinner dance at Old Trafford stadium.

Back row; Joseph Niland, Alex Murdoch, Ryan Brown, Alex Clarke and Tom Cohen. Front row; Liam Kildunne, Dylan Wilde and Adrian Holmes

Kevin and Pauline Archer with Tony and Samantha Cagney.

Sandra and Kevin Regan, Leona Carolan, Niall O'Donaghue and Tommy Halligan.

Thomas Halligan, Kieran Gaughan, Siobhan Halligan and friends.

ST ANN'S SCHOOL, BERNIE WHITE (NÉE O'BRIEN)

When I walk into St Ann's Club I always feel at home and a part of the history of the parish. Even when I attend a function in the social centre, walking into my late aunt's classroom which is where the main room is, all the memories come back of the formidable Miss O'Brien and the many stories I have heard from past pupils of her days at St Ann's – some happy, some sad, some good, some not so good!

Miss O'Brien spent thirty years at St Ann's and finished as deputy head of the infants where Mrs Baguley was the headmistress. In Miss O'Brien's early days in the reception class she would have fifty children in her care and her proudest boast was that no child ever left her class without being able to read. She was strict but fair and even now, when people realise I am her niece, there are no shortage of memories to be shared. I am often reminded of the wendy house in the corner of the room where naughty children would be sent to sit in solitude and reflect on their behaviour.

As a child I often visited her classroom which had an open fire in the corner with a fireguard around, often with damp underwear drying! The caretaker, Mr Vin Moss who lived near the school on Trafford Grove, would often call into the classroom and sit by the fire smoking! Incredible considering the regulations and health and safety rules these days – but the children were still happy and learned to read and write. St Ann's was a happy school and after the infants the children would move on to the junior school where Maurice Taylor was the head and oversaw more happy years in the school.

The GAA club is an integral part of the community which I know she would approve of. After leaving the school she spent many happy years helping out at the St Ann's over-sixties club. Her funeral in September 2003 at St Ann's Church was a month before the first St Ann's GAA dinner dance and was attended by many parishioners, past pupils and the church was full – surprising for a ninety-year-old who had outlived most of her friends.

Anne O'Brien with a group of children going to First Holy Communion, c. 1977.

8

SPORT

This football picture is of Jack O'Brien, back row, third from left, from 1948 with pupils from Old Trafford boys school.

In 1986 Aran Travel sponsored a nine-a-side hurling competition. Pictured here are the Sarsfield Gaels hurlers who defeated St Kentigern's in the final. On the extreme right is the late Jim Phelan of Aran Travel.

St Lawrence's GAA Club under-10s team, 1984.

Oisin GAA Club's under-16s team, 1985.

The St Kentigern's GAA football team, 1985.

The St Richard's GAA football team, 1985.

The Lancashire under-21s team which beat London in the 1998 All-Britain provincial final at Hough End Fields in Manchester.

The Irish World Heritage Centre's cycling club are pictured here in 1991 ready to set off on a ride. Seen here are Jason Whelehan, Frank Boucher, Tommie Whelehan, Sean Reynolds, Michael Forde and Michael Forde Jnr, Danny Molloy and Brian Kennedy.

In 1994 St Michael's Amateur Boxing Club came over from Athy in County Kildare to take part in a boxing tournament at the Grove Club. Pictured here are Tony Sheehan from Athy and a sixteen-year-old lad called Richard Hatton representing Manchester. He was later better known as Ricky Hatton and went on to be a world champion.

Members of the Donegal Association's darts team which won the Manchester Irish Sports Indoor League darts competition at the Irish World Heritage Centre in December 1998.

Members of Emerald Gaels Ladies GAA Club are pictured here at a celebration dance held in the Grove Club, December 1996. They had just become All Britain and Provincial Ladies Gaelic football champions.

Fr Pat Clarke runs a mission in Brazil for the street children in the city of São Paulo. Each year relatives and friends organise a fundraising night in Manchester to help him in his very important work. Fr Pat is pictured here left with Manchester City footballer Niall Quinn, his great friend Fr John Ahern and Dominic Mulcahy at a fundraiser in the Irish Association Club in 1991.

This is the Oisin's senior team celebrating after having beaten St Brendan's in the Lancashire senior final at Houghend Fields to become champions of 1994. They also became the All-Britain senior champions and received an Irish Post Award in the same year.

St Brendan's GAA Club's under-12s team that had just clinched the Lancashire Championship in 1998.

Celebrating at the St Brendan's GAA dinner in 1991 is the successful ladies football team.

Young Oisin GAA Club footballers at a presentation disco in 1984.

A group of children taking part in the sack race at the St Brendan's GAA sports day in 1990.

Oisin under-10s presentation night at Old Bedians in November 1996.

In 1986 this team comprised mainly Irish players who represented the Manchester YMCA Club in the North-West Counties Squash League and won at their first attempt. Here we see Martin Quirke, Alan Tallantire, Jim Collins (Mayo), Eamon Quirke (Galway), Paddy and Linda Darnbrough (both Dublin), and Joe Rush (Mayo).

At a Republic of Ireland Soccer Supporters' Club meeting at the 32 Club in 1995. Jimmy and Sheila Callaghan, Kevin McNeill and Suzanne O'Hara (now married).

Presentation night at the Manchester Irish Sports Association, 1988.

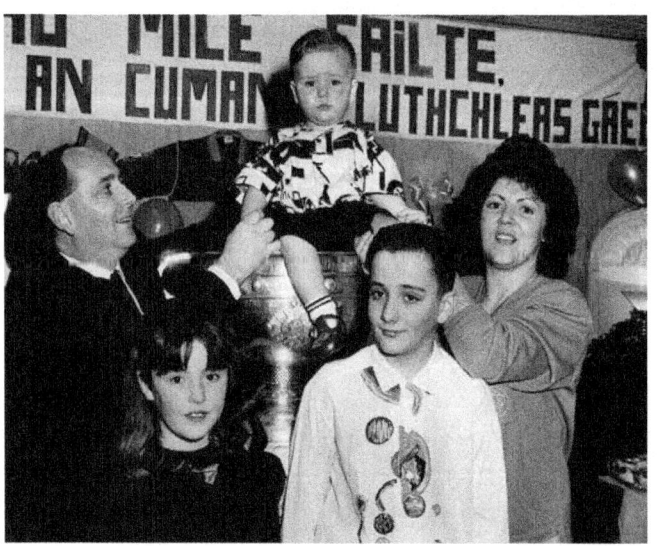

Donegal were the All Ireland Senior Champions in 1992/93 and brought the Sam Maguire Cup over to Manchester in February 1993. The photo was taken at the Fiddler's Green pub in Levenshulme, both the landlord James Rodden and his wife Bridie come from Donegal. They are pictured here with their three children. Sitting in the Sam Maguire Cup is young Seimi, with his sister Mairead and brother Paul at front.

9

PEOPLE & PLACES

Eamon de Valera unveiling the monument to Fenian soldier Seamus Barrett at Moston Cemetery in 1948.

Piping guests into mass with Corpus Christi flute band at St Patrick's Church, Livesey Street, Collyhurst, in memory of the Manchester Martyrs in 1948.

St Chad's junior school in Cheetham Hill which had a large Irish intake over the years.

Priests from St Wilfrid's Church in Hulme stepping out in style in the 1940s.

Charlie Gildea and Pat Feeley, a painter and a joiner working on a Manchester building site in the mid-1960s.

Nora Walsh and Eileen Kearns, both Dublin girls, working in the laundry of Manchester Royal Eye Hospital in the early 1950s.

The wedding party of Ann and John Bohan in Cecil Street, Chorlton-on-Medlock, 30 December 1950. Ann (from Mayo) and John (from Leitrim) were married at St Joseph's Church on Plymouth Grove in Longsight.

Six hardworking Irishmen pictured here at the coalface of Ashton Moss Colliery in the mid-1960s. They are Tim Finnerty, Dominic Stenson, Danny Regan, Martin Dillon, Jim Lavin and Jimmy Golden.

In March 1986 well-known Galway man Michael Griffin and his wife Babe from Mayo celebrated their silver wedding anniversary with a big party for family and friends. They are pictured here with their six sons, Michael, Peter, John, Gerard, Fintan and Robert.

Enjoying a night out at the Chorlton Irish Club in July 1995 are Mike Kedian, Tom Brett, Mike Hassall, Sarah Leeming, Sean and Jo Brett.

Members of the St Wilfrid's Branch of Comhaltas presented their play *The Matchmaker* in 1986. The Matchmaker in the tall hat was played by Donegal man Pat Sweeney who later went on to become President of Comhaltas Ceoltoiri Eireanne.

Pictured here at the opening of the Cheetham Hill office of Irish Community Care back in February 1991 are Fr John Ahern and Bertie Aherne who eventually went on to become Taoiseach of Ireland.

Future Taoiseach Bertie Aherne poses for a photograph with Irish Community Care workers and volunteers at a meeting in the Irish World Heritage Centre while he was over to open the new Irish Community Care office in February 1991.

Joining in the Irish Association's silver jubilee celebrations in June 1985 are Martin Flynn; Michael, Catherine, Mike and Mary O'Dwyer; Simon Cunliffe; Mamie O'Dwyer; Maureen Doohan and John Kennedy.

Enjoying a night out at the Tara Club in the 1950s. Back row, left to right: Tommie and Ciss Lynch, Charlie Gallagher, Jimmy Monagle, Pat Walsh and Mary Gallogly. Front row: Nellie Murphy, Sonny Bohan, Margaret Bohan and John Bohan.

Enjoying a ceili in Bolton Irish Centre in 1996 are John Burke, Jim McSharry and Brendan O'Doherty.

Enjoying a Bolton Irish Society dinner at the Packhorse Hotel in Bolton in 1991 are Peggy Fiske, Pat Callaghan, Josie and Phillip Gargan.

Martin Ruane, who was better known all over the world as wrestler Giant Haystacks, is pictured here on the right with his wife Rita and Bill Stephens. The photograph was taken in May 1998 in the English Martyrs Parish Centre when Bill organised a dance to raise funds to fight Lymphoma. Martin, whose family came from Mayo, was delighted to help out on the night as he himself was in remission from cancer at the time. Sadly his cancer returned and Martin died exactly six months later on 29 November at the age of fifty-two.

Back in the 1960s, sunny summer afternoons in Platt Fields Park were always popular with the young Irish community in Manchester. It was a great place to meet friends, and perhaps catch the eye of a new girlfriend or boyfriend. Among this happy group are Pat Feeley, Paddy O'Malley, Brendan Molloy, Seamus Feeley and Paddy Joe Walsh.

A popular Irish shop in the early 1990s was Pat's Corner, which was situated on the corner of Platt Lane and Wilmslow Road in Rusholme. It was run by Mayo man Pat Conway who would sell you anything from spuds to videos and more besides.

Photographed at a West of Ireland reunion dance at the Grove Club in 1993 are Helen Dinan, Sandra Cox, Mike Regan, Josie Miskell and Yvonne McColgan.

Longford couple Paddy and Rose McNally celebrated their silver wedding anniversary at the 32 Club back in 1990. Rose and Paddy are pictured here centre with their family, Paul, Shaun, Jacqueline and Greg.

President Mary Robinson on a visit to Ashton-under-Lyne in February 1997.

A new Irish landmark opened in the city centre in May 1994 – O'Shea's pub on the corner of Princess Street and Whitworth Street. Pictured here at a party to celebrate O'Shea's first birthday in May 1995 are Mike Walsh, Noel Hill, Sean Woods, Marcus Barke, Damien McMenamin and Jenny Barker.

The finalists in the 1997 Manchester Rose of Tralee competition that was held at the Grove Club. The winner was Siobhan Madden who represented the Chorlton Irish Club (fourth from the left on the back row).

The finalists in the 1998 Rose of Tralee competition at the Grove Club. The winner was Liverpudlian Anne-Marie Mohan (second from the right on the back row.)

Chris O'Connor, Alan Keegan, Lawrence Hennigan and Greg McNally at the launch of Manchester Irish Radio in 1994 outside the Palace nightclub.

At the launch of Manchester Irish Festival Radio in 1999 at Manchester Town Hall are John Commons, Daniel O'Donnell and Kathleen Waldron.

Children enjoying the Christmas party at the Irish Association Club, Chorlton, 1984.

In 1996 Joe Kennedy celebrated his sixtieth birthday at a special party for family and friends in Prestbury. Joe is pictured here with his family on the night.

Pat and Eileen McGuinness and Jeanette, Patricia and Jim Devery celebrating at the St Patrick's Society dinner at the Palace Hotel on St Patrick's night, 1997.

Irish Association annual dinner held at the Piccadilly Hotel including some of the original founders in the late 1960s or early 1970s.

Irish Association dinner dance, possibly at the Grand Hotel, Manchester, 1966. Monsignor Sewell, Kathleen Kennedy, Joe Kennedy, Paddy Curley (standing), Mary Curley, Bernadette Robinson, George Robinson.

The men line up for a photograph at the Irish Association's annual dinner at the Hotel Piccadilly in January 1998.

At the National Federation of Demolition Contractors AGM in London, seen here with the Federation Patron Lord Snowdon (seated) are, left to right: Adrian Kelly (Windmill Demolition), Peter O'Connor (P.P. O'Connor Ltd), Jim Connell (Connell Bros Ltd), Patrick Williamson, John Connell (Connell Bros Ltd), Tom McDonnell (Westway Demolition), Andrew Connolly, Mark Bryan, Barry Connell (Connell Bros Ltd) and Dave Hoyle.

The Parlour team won the annual Mayo Association award in 2005 for their splendid work over the years with their popular radio programme on the local BBC. Pictured here are Julie Keegan, Ged Hynes, Simon Greene, Sam Healey, Gemma Fitzmaurice, Ian Barrie, Bill Sweeney, P.J. Kinsella, Natalie Bedford, Michael Forde, Evelyn Grealy. Michael Kierans is seen in the middle holding the award and knealing at the front are Eamon O'Neal and Alan Keegan.

JIM CHRISTIE

In 1971 I was a young lad of seventeen living in Belfast. Things in Northern Ireland were bad, the troubles were spreading all over the city, so my mother and father, Eva and Joe, thought it would be safer to move over to England. We soon settled down in Manchester and that first week we all got jobs; dad (who was from Belfast) working for John Laing, mum (who was from Ballaghaderreen, County Roscommon) worked in Withington at Duncan and Fosters bakery, and I got a job at the Portland bars, under the Piccadilly Hotel.

I had six happy years working there, then one Thursday night in the bar, someone had left the *Manchester Evening News* on the bar, so I had a read of the jobs section and saw an advert for driving instructors. I had a long think about it, and the next day I went to their office. They asked if I could go to London to start training on Monday for a week and so I went for it. All went well with the training and I passed. I stayed with them for three years and had a great time, then I decided to set up by myself, so on 8 October 1980, I started the Jim Christie School of Motoring. I had a Mini Metro to begin with, but that didn't last too long with all the work that was coming  in, so the next car I got was a 1981 red Triumph Acclaim, a very nice car as you can see. A few days later I was washing my car in the driveway, when this lovely girl called Denise O'Connor, who lived seven doors away, stopped and said to me, 'I love your car.' An hour later she was still there. Three years later we were married. I would like to thank all the people of Manchester, especially all the Irish, because without them I would be no one; I have never had to advertise for over thirty years – it was all done with word of mouth.

MARGARET AND TOMMIE CASSERLEY (BY JOE CASSERLEY)

In 1960 Margaret and Tommie Casserley arrived in Birmingham where Tommie had been offered the opportunity of a job. After five years' hard work and two children, Leo and Joe, they headed north to Manchester to be closer to Margaret's family. With their love for music and dancing it wasn't long before they became regular members of the Irish Association Social Club in Chorlton where they made many friends. Margaret also had a talent for singing and Tommie played the drums. 1970 saw the arrival of their third child, Lorraine.

With their children grown up, Margaret and Tommie joined forces with other exiles from their native county to form the Manchester Roscommon Association in 1985 which quickly became one of the biggest in Manchester with 800 people attending their first dinner dance in the Kings Hall in Belle Vue. The 1990s were a busy time as Margaret became the stewardess of the 104 Club in Withington and her and husband Tommie took their love for music to the airwaves with a weekly show called *The Casserleys* on the hugely popular Manchester Irish Festival Radio. In 2001 Margaret left the 104 Club when she was diagnosed with breast cancer from which she made a full recovery and became the stewardess of local sports club Old Bedians in Didsbury. It was also the start of her crusade (along with the Roscommon Association) to raise as much money as possible for local charities and in particular Christies for Cancer who have treated both Margaret and Tommie. In 2004 Margaret joined her son Joe on his weekly radio show, *The Full Irish* on All FM, where she still helps today. 2011 was once again a very difficult year as Margaret suffered an aneurism, but we are pleased to say she is on the road to recovery.

Manchester Whit Walks, 1954. Margaret Mcloughlin is in the centre walking from Ardwick to Piccadilly Gardens.

Margaret McLoughlin (not Casserley yet), Kathleen and Luke Mullin (landlord and landlady of the Black Horse pub on Greek Street in All Saints, Manchester) with their two children James and Imelda, photographed in the Black Horse, 1953.

The Union of Catholic Mothers outside St John's RC Church, High Lane, Chorlton.

Michael and Maureen Martin with Margaret and Tommie Casserley at the Irish Association dinner dance in the Piccadilly Hotel in the mid-1970s.

The Union of Catholic Mothers again. Here we see Mrs Kilcommons, Mrs Griffin, Margaret Casserley, Mary McNulty, Margaret Johnson, Teresa O'Donoghue (a teacher at St John's School) Joan Constable, Marry Mills, Phil Finn, Eta O'Mara, Frances Mullooly, Teresa Kenney, Nora Paddock and Madeline Chiles, 1970s.

Michael Butler, chair of the Roscommon Association with Bishop Conway from Elphin and Austin Smith at the Armitage Centre, Fallowfield, 1980s.

Jim Kenny, Bridie Taylor, Tommie Casserley, Ollie and Francis Mullooly, Teresa Kenny, Margaret Casserley, Margaret Chapman and Delia (barmaid), 1983.

Margaret and Tommie at the Chorlon Irish club in 1985 with Johnny Sice (of Johnny and the Sunsets) at the microphone.

Tommie and Margaret Casserley with Tom Grogan on their radio show *Down Memory Lane with the Casserleys* on Manchester Irish Festival Radio, which broadcast from Manchester Town Hall in the 1990s.

How's the Craic?: an outside radio broadcast from the Grove Club, Plymouth Grove, 1980s.

Margaret and Tommie Casserley celebrate their silver wedding anniversary with family and friends in 1985. This photograph was taken in the lounge of the Irish Association Club, Chorlton.

Margaret and Tommie with friends at a Roscommon Association event at the Irish Association Club in Chorlton.

ACKNOWLEDGEMENTS

The following helped in various ways or loaned and gave permission to reproduce photographs:

P. Curley, J. and B. Connell, R. Morris, J. Casserley, M. Waldron, A. Murphy, B. White, J. Kennedy, N. Walsh, M. and N. Burke, Pat Feeley, Rose Duffy, the Grainger family, the Sweeney family, the Stenson family, S. Keegan, D. Costello, M. Butler, T. Finnigan, the Hennigan family, T. Coogan, H. Keegan, M. Cagney, M. Keegan, P. Rafter, the Griffin family, M. Casserley, J. Keegan, Ian Penney, P. Fitzpatrick, A. Bohan Taghian, E. Lally, the Breen family and Manchester Archives and Local Studies, Central Library, Manchester.

Thanks also to friends and colleagues at the University of Central Lancashire, Preston, and the team at The History Press, especially Michelle Tilling and Richard Leatherdale.

Sincere thanks to each and every one, and apologies for any omissions or errors which may have crept in at the last minute. The responsibility is entirely ours.

Please continue to send us your Irish memories, stories and photographs:
info@irishmanchester.com
www.facebook.com/irishmanchester

Printed in Dunstable, United Kingdom